Action Learning in Schools

D0139760

Teaching is becoming increasingly complex in the twenty-first century, creating a need for more sophisticated frameworks to support teachers' professional learning. Action learning is one such framework and has been used for workplace learning in business settings for many years. It is now becoming increasingly popular in school and university settings, but it is often misunderstood. This book clarifies what action learning is, linking key concepts to illustrate that it is not merely a process, but a dynamic interaction among professional learning, communities, leadership and change. The book brings together more than a decade of the authors' research in school-based action learning.

Rich and diverse, the research draws on more than one hundred case studies of action learning by teams of teachers in schools. The authors:

- provide practical advice on how to initiate and sustain action learning;
- explain the interaction between action learning, teacher development, professional learning, community building, leadership and change; and
- illustrate how action learning can link to classroom practice so closely that it becomes part of what teachers *do*, rather than an added impost.

Addressing the highs and lows, the successes and failures, and their underlying causes, *Action Learning in Schools* provides insights into theories of cooperation, innovation, leadership and community formation to inform individual projects and large-scale school improvement initiatives. It will be of interest to teacher educators, pre-service and experienced teachers alike, as well as school and education system managers and policymakers keen to enhance teacher professional learning and educational outcomes for students.

Peter Aubusson is Associate Professor in Education and Head of Teacher Education Programs at the University of Technology, Sydney.

Robyn Ewing is Professor of Teacher Education and the Arts and Acting Dean in the Faculty of Education and Social Work at the University of Sydney.

Garry Hoban is Associate Professor of Science Education and Teacher Education at the University of Wollongong.

Action Learning in Schools

Reframing teachers' professional learning and development

Peter Aubusson, Robyn Ewing and Garry Hoban

Routledge
Taylor & Francis Group

LONDON AND NEW YORK

First published 2009
by Routledge
2 Park Square, Milton Park, Abingdon, Oxon OX14 4RN

Simultaneously published in the USA and Canada
by Routledge
29 West 35th Street, New York, NY 10001

Routledge is an imprint of the Taylor & Francis Group, an informa business

© 2009 Peter Aubusson, Robyn Ewing and Garry Hoban

Typeset in Garamond by
Florence Production Ltd, Stoodleigh, Devon
Printed and bound in Great Britain by
TJ International Ltd, Padstow, Cornwall

British Library Cataloguing in Publication Data
A catalogue record for this book is available from the British Library

Library of Congress Cataloging in Publication Data
Aubusson, Peter.
   Action learning in schools: reframing teachers' professional learning
   and development/Peter Aubusson, Robyn Ewing, Garry Hoban.
      p. cm.
   Includes index.
   1. Teachers – In-service training.   2. Active learning.
   I. Ewing, Robyn.   II. Hoban, Garry F. (Garry Francis), 1953–.
   III. Title.
LB1731.A85 2009
370.71'5–dc22   2008054632

ISBN10: 0–415–47514–7 (hbk)
ISBN10: 0–415–47515–5 (pbk)

ISBN13: 978–0–415–47514–3 (hbk)
ISBN13: 978–0–415–47515–0 (pbk)

Contents

Acknowledgements

We have drawn on over ten years of research in writing this book. We acknowledge the involvement that our co-researchers over the years have made to this body of work including: Judy Anderson, Michael Anderson, Laurie Brady, Sue Butler, Val Burton, Steve Dinham, Annette Gard, Robyn Gibson, Janette Griffin, Robyn Griffiths, Geoff Hastings, Tony Herrington, Loraine Lesslie, Lisa Kervin, David Lloyd, Craig Luccarda, Jackie Manuel, John Morris, Irene O'Brien, David Smith and Fran Steele. In addition, the warm welcome and ongoing support of many teachers in schools have been extremely important. Ethics provisions prevent us naming them, but we remain forever grateful to them for their trust, professionalism and frankness. Many research assistants have made contributions over the years, and we thank them for their commitment and input.

We acknowledge the funding from the NSW Department of Education and Training and the Australian Government Quality Teaching Programme that enabled some of our research to take place. We particularly thank Frances Plummer for her commitment to, and support for, school-based professional learning. Without her assistance many teachers with whom we have worked would never have engaged with action learning. We also acknowledge the contribution made by our colleagues at the University of Sydney, the University of Technology, Sydney and the University of Wollongong for their generous feedback on papers, seminars and ideas over many fruitful and often robust conversations.

The production of the book itself has been made possible by the support and assistance of many people. We particularly acknowledge the significant role of Steve Dinham in the development of the book proposal, in early drafts and his contribution in Chapter 3: Enabling action learning. We are very grateful to John Furlong for his generous contribution of the Foreword. For their assistance with many aspects of early drafts and diagrams we thank Daniel Brooks and Margaret McComb. Several people kindly read over sections of the book, making suggestions and comments that have much improved it. Finally, for their tireless work in editing, suggesting changes, locating references, formatting and doing the thousands of things that needed to be done, sincere thanks to Kate Aubusson and Sarah Buultjens.

Foreword

John Furlong

In the last few years, we have learned a great deal about what strategies best support effective professional learning for teachers. This is because governments in a number of countries, including Australia, the USA and the UK, have commissioned systematic reviews of research that has evaluated different approaches to in-service education for the teaching profession. The consistent findings of these reviews show that, if they are to be effective, programmes first need be sustained; one-off seminars and workshops can be useful to give an initial impetus to the introduction of new ideas, but they can only begin to transform practice if they are designed as part of a sustained programme of support and challenge as the teachers seek to implement those ideas. Professional development programmes also need to be collaborative. The evidence is quite clear that new understandings are only likely to become embedded in school practice if teachers work together in teams. This means more than passing on ideas from attendance at a briefing or workshop. As well as discussion, it involves such activities as shared planning and resource design, peer observation and analysis.

While we may know what an effective professional development programme looks like, we also know that the reality is often very different. A recent 'state of the nation' survey by McCormick *et al.* (forthcoming) of teachers' experiences of professional development programmes in England demonstrated, yet again, that most of the programmes offered to teachers in that country remain 'top-down', short-term events; they are nearly always disconnected from teachers' own school contexts, and most offer no opportunities for collaboration. As a result, it is not surprising that the study found that the majority of teachers do not rate their professional development experiences particularly highly. There is little evidence here that what governments now know is actually being put into practice.

It is for this reason that I particularly welcome this book on action learning. Action learning is based on the idea that a key strategy in supporting professional learning must be to engage groups of professionals themselves in their own work-based learning. It involves creating a learning environment where small groups of professionals can come together to seek answers to questions that are relevant to them and their needs. As the authors say, action learning provides a means to create new possibilities for change, using the resources of the people who know best – the teachers in the schools. It recognises the capacities of teachers with expertise and knowledge of their particular school contexts, which must be understood if innovation is to succeed.

Action learning of course is not a new idea. As this book documents, it has a long history stretching back to the 1940s, initially in business settings. And its use is not confined to schools; as a strategy to support professional learning, it has been used successfully in a wide range of different contexts – industry, the health service, even among a group of foremen in the Williams Grand Prix racing team. But, as an approach, it has not yet become embedded in mainstream schooling; that is why this book is needed. What the authors provide for the first time is a clear rationale for using action learning in schools, as well as practical advice on how it can be introduced effectively to support whole-school learning.

In our rapidly changing society, innovation, development and reform are part of everyday life – in schools as elsewhere. That means that everyone involved in schools has to engage in continuous professional learning; it is what 'being professional' must now mean. However, many efforts for educational reform are short lived precisely because they are not accompanied by processes and conditions to support teacher learning. As the authors of this book argue so convincingly, if developed effectively, action learning provides the learning processes and conditions to underpin the longevity of professional learning reform and increase the possibilities for change, thereby enhancing the quality of learning our schools can offer to children.

Chapter 1

Our remedies oft in ourselves do lie[*]

Introduction

Action learning has been used for workplace learning in business organisations for over seventy years, but it is only in the last fifteen years that it has been applied in schools to underpin teachers' professional learning. It is timely that the value of action learning is explored in this book as a contribution to teacher learning and development literature. In this book we have examined the roles, processes and outcomes of action learning in school contexts, bringing together more than a decade of our research in action learning projects.

Our research includes projects we have conducted using action learning, as well as studies of school-based action learning conducted by teams of teachers. The research projects discussed are rich and diverse, while they also share the common goal of sustaining teacher professional learning to improve classroom practice. We have drawn on more than a hundred case studies of action learning in schools. Many of these involve teachers collaborating with academic partners to facilitate action learning. By analysing these case studies, we explain how action learning interacts with teacher development, professional learning, community building, sustaining change and school-based innovation. In the busy world of teaching, action learning can link closely to classroom practice so that it becomes part of what teachers do rather than an added imposition.

It will also be shown that understanding how action learning works and how it can be organised is critical to its ongoing success, so that it does not fail just as it germinates. This book describes the successes and failures of action learning, and suggests some of their underlying causes. It provides practical advice on when, how and why to initiate and sustain action learning. It articulates theories of teacher learning underpinning action learning, as well as notions of teacher professionalism that can inform individual projects and large-scale innovations.

This book also spans significant fields of educational development to illustrate action learning, not merely as a process for implementation, but as a dynamic and interactive tool that can link the teacher learning processes of reflection, community, leadership, action and feedback. Action learning

[*] Shakespeare, *All's well that ends well*, Act I, Scene I.

is a process at all levels, not just because it requires team members to respect each other in their professional conversations, but also because it acknowledges and utilises the creativity, wisdom and practice of teachers as professionals.

While traditional debates about school improvement have focused on a dichotomy of top-down/bottom-up approaches, we believe action learning can span the apparent differences in these approaches. Action learning provides a framework to address the many challenges, problems, issues and concerns that arise in schools. For example, in a school, the problem of poor student engagement might be addressed by implementing a well-known pedagogical approach such as cooperative learning. Like many attempts to address such problems, teachers face the question of how to arrive at the desired outcome. The problem is not one of what is to be done, but how to get it done. In this situation, action learning can be used as a process to find ways to implement the new approach in the school to improve student engagement. Alternatively, the same goal to improve student engagement may be achieved by a different pathway, depending on the context of the school. Action learning provides a means to create new possibilities for change, using the resources of the people who know best: the teachers in the schools. Action learning recognises the capacities of teachers with expertise and knowledge of their particular school contexts, which must be understood if innovation is to succeed. Action learning that succeeds works because it is a collaborative learning process that does not presuppose that the means to an end are available a priori, and because it assumes that problems in real schools require professionals to learn *in situ* if practical, productive change in education is to be realised.

If the potential of action learning in education is to be realised, then its underlying principles need to be clearly understood and its practices explained. The book explains in depth the key aspects of action learning in schools. The chapter entitled 'Positioning action learning' discusses the fundamental character of action learning and explores its place in teacher learning, school innovation and change. The chapter begins by examining the origins of action learning in the writing of Revans in the 1940s, as he worked with the managers of coal-mines to share and find solutions to their management problems. It outlines action learning as a professional learning framework and illustrates this framework using examples in various industries and the public sector. This chapter also clarifies the differences between action learning and action research, as well as between professional development and professional learning.

Having established a prima facie case for action learning as a vehicle for professional learning and innovation in schools, the next chapter, 'Enabling action learning: Getting started', explains how to initiate and promote action learning in a school setting. Taking into account the external factors that influence individual schools, including socio-political contexts, this chapter explains how action learning can be instigated to target real issues of significance to particular school communities. Matters considered include: selecting, defining and focusing the issue, concern or problem; setting targets and timelines; the type of leadership required to promote action learning; team formation, membership and shared responsibility; and meeting the challenges of applying action learning in school environments.

Consideration of how to initiate and plan for action learning leads naturally to an analysis of the principles and practices that underpin it. 'The dynamics of action learning' expounds the four key processes of action learning to show how they interrelate and enhance each other. The first process, reflection, involves participants thinking about something problematic to make sense of their experiences and help them cope with similar situations in the future. The second process, community, involves a group of six to eight members sharing personal anecdotes to gain a deeper understanding of the meaning of their personal experiences. The third process, action, entails participants exploring ideas that have been generated by personal reflection and community discussions. And the fourth process, feedback, utilises the important element of responses to actions from colleagues and students. Independently, these principles are not new, but action learning is a framework that integrates all four processes to create a dynamic relationship, providing a helpful mechanism to support ongoing professional learning.

The following chapter on 'Community' elaborates on the synergistic interactions between action learning and community. This chapter offers insight into ways that the building of community can be enhanced. It discusses different views of professional community and learning teams to highlight implications for using action learning in schools. Barriers to community formation are discussed in the context of ways action learning can assist to overcome them. It is also acknowledged that, just as the genesis of a professional learning community can lie in action learning, so too the existence of a collaborative school community can lay the foundation for the origin and evolution of action learning.

Effective, evolving professional communities are not isolated but have mechanisms to generate new ideas from within, as well as ways to allow new ideas to enter from outside. One device that supports this in action learning is the external facilitator. The chapter on 'Facilitating action learning: The academic partner's role' is divided into two sections, examining two aspects of external assistance to schools during an action learning project. It begins by briefly examining the role that system personnel can provide through external assistance in funding, framing and developing parameters to support action learning. The main part of the chapter then explores the crucial role that an external partner can play as a critical friend in school-based action learning. Both action learning team and academic partner perspectives are discussed, and some frameworks for working productively are suggested, based on our experiences.

'Gathering and learning from evidence' builds on previous chapters, arguing that action learning depends on professional conversation from a committed team of teachers. The basis for the team's decision-making and learning can be shifted to more robust ways of thinking by seeking evidence to inform these conversations. The chapter explores the ways in which teachers gather evidence in action learning, how this is analysed, and how it is used to inform or promote innovation. It also discusses peer observation, the selection and use of instruments, survey, focused discussions, reflection, reporting, capturing episodes, stories, anecdotes and the role of professional sharing. While acknowledging the role of these elements in research, this chapter focuses on the part they play in, and what it means to engage in, professional learning with colleagues.

Rich conversation, the honest sharing of views, trust and genuine collaboration are integral to action learning. This requires much of our personal and professional selves – our beliefs, values and practices – to be exposed to others. It also leads to actions that can have significant consequences for others. These matters raise significant ethical questions for action learning. Yet, to date, the ethics of action learning in schools have been largely ignored in the literature. The chapter on 'Ethical action learning' explains what it means to be ethical in action learning by considering the consequences of our actions for others.

As a professional learning framework, action learning promotes innovation and change in schools. These are needed to ensure they maintain their key role in our rapidly changing society. However, many efforts for educational reform are short lived because they are not accompanied by processes and conditions to support teacher learning. If developed effectively, action learning provides the learning processes and conditions to underpin the longevity of professional learning reform and to increase the possibilities for change. Our chapter on 'Sustaining professional learning' proposes a model for sustainable professional learning in schools and elaborates the implications for organisational learning. It draws heavily on case studies of projects that have been sustained over three or more years and advocates the establishment of a broad and collaborative professional learning community.

Finally, in the Epilogue 'Extending action learning', we reflect on the complex environment of modern schools and emphasise the need for schools to redesign themselves if they are to maintain relevance in the twenty-first century. Children are rapidly changing in our complex world. Teachers also need to change. This chapter discusses the way in which action learning can help to reinvigorate schools by promoting teacher professionalism and bringing new ideas and practices to the fore. The quality of student learning in schools is dependent on the quality of teacher learning. In concluding, we have speculated on how action learning itself might develop in the future as it continues to fulfil the role of supporting teachers' professional learning.

Chapter 2

Positioning action learning

> Each manager learned not only much about coal mining by discussing his experiences of it with others who were then urged to discuss their own, but he also learned about himself, and why he said the kinds of things he did say; why he felt as he did about the things he did say; why he felt as he did about the decisions as a manager that he could be seen by his own staff and colleagues to take – even if they were bad ones. Action learning, in other words by being question-based rather than answer-based (as in most other training) tells managers a lot about themselves; they begin to see how it is that their own personality is stamped upon the mine they are appointed to run.
>
> (Revans, 1982b: 66)

When Reg Revans, the founder of action learning, wrote these words in 1982 he was arguing that the most valuable type of learning for mine managers involved them reflecting upon workplace experiences and sharing these insights with other managers to help each of them interpret and inform their experiences. This is how action learning started over seventy years ago – by having a small group of people, who worked in similar occupations, give opinions on each other's work-related issues and problems. Moreover, workplace learning is not just about reflection on experiences, as learning from experience means 'action *and* reflection; one gets to understand by doing and to do by understanding' (Revans, 1983b: 49). Emphatically, Revans italicised 'and' because of the essential interplay between the 'doing' (the action) and 'thinking about the consequences of doing' (the reflection) to maximise workplace learning.

Reflection is a process that helps develop meaning from experiences. If you don't reflect, then what you learn from your experiences is limited. This interplay between reflection and experience also resonates with earlier ideas in Dewey's theory of learning through experience (Dewey, 1933) and later in Kolb's notion of experiential learning (Kolb, 1984). While the notion of rethinking actions was first mentioned by Aristotle over two thousand years ago, Dewey (1933) was the first to highlight the value of reflection as a way of thinking about a problematic situation that needs to be resolved: 'The function of reflective thought is, therefore, to transform a situation in which there is experienced obscurity, doubt, conflict, disturbance of some sort, into a situation that is clear, coherent, settled, harmonious' (Dewey, 1933: 100–1).

Although Revans first wrote about action learning in October 1945 in a report commissioned by the Mining Association of Great Britain, he also acknowledged that many of the key ideas underpinning action learning can be found in the writings of Aristotle two thousand years earlier: 'Life, as Aristotle still reminds some of us, is made up of action as well as of reflection' (Revans, 1983b: 50). What Revans did, however, in his original writings, was not only re-emphasise the age-old importance of learning through action and reflection, but demonstrate how it could operate in the workplace. He initially did this by establishing small groups of coal-mine managers to work together to solve each other's operational and management problems (Revans, 1983b).

As this shows, action learning originated in business settings and has evolved in different forms over the last seventy years. It has only been used in schools in the last two decades. The purpose of this chapter, therefore, is to explain the origins of action learning in business settings, clarify what it is, and introduce how it can be used in schools for teachers' professional learning. Since most action learning studies have been conducted in business settings, many of the references in this chapter will come from the literature of this context.

This chapter is presented in four sections. First, we will discuss how different conceptualisations of teaching align with different forms of teacher learning. Second, three different forms of teacher learning will be explained. In this section we will clarify the differences between three common phrases used in the teacher learning literature – 'professional development/in-service', 'continuous professional development' and 'professional learning'. Importantly, we will also articulate the difference between two professional learning frameworks – action learning and action research. Third, examples of action learning will be provided to show that it has already had widespread use in many non-educational settings. Finally, this chapter will argue that teachers should be encouraged to use action learning in schools.

Conceptions of teaching

There is a relationship between the nature of teaching and the type of teacher learning required. From extensive research with teachers in Chicago in the 1980s, Wise et al. (1984) deduced several different conceptions of teaching that necessitate different forms of teacher learning. One conception of teaching suggests that it is a 'craft', meaning that the knowledge base for teaching is fixed and has little to do with varying contexts. This conception implies that teaching is about the delivery of prescribed knowledge and, if teachers can learn enough knowledge about their practice, then it can be 'mastered'. If this is the case, then teachers can learn about their practice 'bit by bit'. This can occur from brief after-school workshops providing different chunks of knowledge about teaching in classrooms.

A different conception of teaching requires a different type of teacher learning. When teaching is viewed as a profession, it implies that the body of knowledge is not fixed, and that what teachers do in classrooms depends on a myriad of factors. This means that teaching is more than the delivery of prescribed knowledge using a range of strategies, but is 'a dynamic relationship that changes with different students and contexts' (Hoban, 2000b: 165). Having a conception of teaching as a profession means that classroom decisions are about many 'holistic judgements' every day (Day, 1999). It means that teaching involves complex decision-making, whereby

> the teacher must draw upon not only a body of professional knowledge and skill, but also a set of personal resources that are uniquely defined and expressed by the personality of the teacher, and his or her individual and collective interactions with students.
>
> (Wise et al., 1984: 8)

Hoyle and John (1995) note that there are three characteristics of being a professional – having knowledge, autonomy and responsibility. This is because

> professionals work in uncertain situations in which judgement is more than routine, it is essential to effective practice that they should be free from bureaucratic and political constraints to act on judgements made in the best interests (as they see them) of the clients.
>
> (Hoyle and John, 1995: 77)

According to McLaughlin (1997: 89), there are six implications for teacher learning if they are to be treated as professionals:

- increasing opportunities for professional dialogue;
- reducing teachers' professional isolation;
- providing a rich menu of nested opportunities for learning and discourse;
- connecting professional development opportunities to meaningful content and change efforts;
- creating an environment of professional safety and trust; and
- restructuring time, space and scale within schools.

In effect, she was talking about schools as learning environments for teachers, so that they can learn more about their own professional contexts. The same point was clearly stated by Sarason (1990), who argued that schools are primarily designed and organised to encourage student learning, with little consideration for teacher learning. He contended that, 'whatever factors, variables, and ambience are conducive for the growth, development, and self-regard of a school's staff are precisely those that are crucial to obtaining the same consequences for students in a classroom' (Sarason, 1990: 154). To consider why schools should be reorganised to encourage long-term teacher learning necessitates understanding the common forms of workplace learning available.

Forms of teacher learning

The terms 'professional development', 'continuing professional development', 'in-service training' and 'professional learning' have been used interchangeably in the teacher learning literature (Craft, 2000). We believe that this has led to some confusion about the characteristics, benefits and usefulness of these different forms of teacher learning. For this reason we distinguish between three types of teacher learning in an attempt to identify their strengths and weaknesses and to explain how they can be used for different reasons and contexts. While teacher learning can occur in all forms, a deeper and more sustained form of learning that can lead to a change in practice is more likely to occur in professional learning than in the other two forms. Although there are examples of teacher learning that use combinations of these forms, they will be treated separately to highlight their distinctive features; however, they are not mutually exclusive.

Professional development/in-service programme

The traditional model of teacher learning in schools for the past fifty years or more has been one of presenting generalised knowledge for teachers to apply in their classrooms in order to solve specific problems of practice (Day, 1999). This form of teacher learning is usually termed a 'professional development programme' and often involves a one-off after-school 'workshop' or one-day 'inservice course' (Hoban and Erickson, 2004). The content of teacher learning is presented in a relatively brief period of time such as in one or two hours after school, and teachers usually have little responsibility in deciding what is presented. The intention is to package the 'accepted knowledge' of a field in a predetermined brief course, with the expectation that practitioners will apply that knowledge in a sensible and proficient manner when they return to their classroom. Moreover, the content of a professional development programme is usually predetermined and, hence, the word 'programme' is apt. This traditional 'stand and deliver' or 'training' model for teacher learning has been the source of substantial debate over the years, leading to well-known phrases such as the 'theory–practice divide'.

The model has also been labelled as a 'technical rational' approach by Schön (1983), whereby 'professional activity consists in instrumental problem solving made rigorous by the application of scientific theory and technique' (Schön, 1983: 21). He argued that this has been the dominant epistemological view of the relationship between formal, disciplinary knowledge and practice for most of the twentieth century.

Traditional professional development has been criticised because it often lacks any systematic support in a school setting to sustain teacher learning after the presentation of the workshop or in-service course. For example, Fullan argued that:

> Professional development for teachers has a poor track record because it lacks a theoretical base and coherent focus. On the one hand, professional development is treated as a vague panacea . . . on the other hand, professional development is defined too narrowly and becomes artificially detached from 'real-time' learning. It becomes the workshop, or possibly an on-going series of professional development sessions. In either case, it fails to have a sustained cumulative impact.
>
> (Fullan, 1993: 253)

Professional development programmes usually occur in the form of a one-off training event, school development day or presentation. This is best exemplified in the typical 'after-school workshop', which is common in school settings today. These are a low-cost form of teacher learning, as no teacher release time is involved and information can be packaged and presented to a group of teachers in one hit, with little follow-up support. Hence, the main factor of this form of teacher learning is the presentation of new information or content to teachers, with little consideration for the context in which they need to apply this new knowledge. Professional development, however, can enhance teacher learning, especially if the content of the workshop matches the teachers' prior knowledge or is complementary to their existing practices. Although there may be some follow-up discussions after the workshop, these are usually ad hoc and do not normally lead to substantive change in practice. Other researchers also have concurred about the inadequacy of one-off workshops to promote teacher learning (Fullan, 1982; 1993). In agreement, Day (1999) maintains that 'professional development opportunities must provide a range of learning experiences which encourage teachers to reflect upon and inquire into their thinking and practice through interaction between their own and others' experiences' (Day, 1999: 201). In some cases, schools may organise their own follow-up support, such as teachers providing feedback to each other and organising ongoing discussions, but this scenario is rare. If teacher learning occurs from a one-off training workshop, it usually reinforces or extends existing practice.

According to Sachs and Logan (1990), a conventional, in-service workshop does not empower teachers to generate their own knowledge:

> Rather than initiating programmes that are intellectually challenging and rigorous, inservice education, with some exceptions, has reproduced current practice by catering for teachers' preoccupation with 'practicality' and 'relevance.' One consequence is that teachers' professional knowledge is being controlled, devalued and deskilled.
>
> (Sachs and Logan, 1990: 479)

In summary, a one-off workshop or professional development day rarely results in a substantive change in practice.

Continuous professional development

A second form of teacher learning has been called 'continuous professional development' (CPD) and involves a series of related workshops, in-service courses, graduate courses or conferences. This form is often used to upgrade qualifications by undertaking a new degree for the purpose of accreditation or a new salary increment. This sequence of professional events means that teachers have the chance to try out some of the ideas in practice and then possibly revisit these when they participate in follow-up courses. Also, new knowledge is often introduced to teachers in the course materials or lectures, and, similar to professional development, teachers have little input into the content of what is presented. Sometimes ongoing workshops or meetings provide opportunities for teachers from different schools to collaborate after the presentations, which enhances possibilities for teacher learning. In contrast to a one-off professional development workshop, continuing professional development is ongoing and may have structures to provide teacher learning processes. However, the content of courses is usually predetermined. Without structures to support teachers in the implementation of new ideas into the school context, the chances of changing teaching practices are reduced.

Research conducted in school settings over the last thirty years has shown that teacher learning is not a simple process (Hoban, 2002). In fact, there is an increasing awareness of the complexity of school classrooms, often characterised by elements of uncertainty, rapid change, value conflicts and dilemmas (Fullan, 1999). Biggs (1993) argued that teachers are reluctant to change their practices because what they do is related to a combination of influences interacting as a 'classroom system' that makes change difficult to occur. He contends that ways of teaching have developed over many years and are usually aligned with existing resources, assessment practices, reporting procedures and policies (both school and state). For example, transmissive teaching approaches, often used by high school mathematics and science teachers, are related to pressures created by a crowded, prescriptive syllabus, limited classroom resources, school reporting procedures that require specific grading and having to teach five or six different classes per day. Elementary teachers have different challenges. Although they usually do not have the pressure of teaching to high-stakes exams, they do have the challenge of teaching all subject areas, sometimes with a very prescriptive syllabus. Introducing a new approach to teachers, therefore, means 'realigning' assessment, resources and existing practices. Of course, this all takes time and energy, which are often in short supply in a busy school. Acknowledging the challenges and pressures teachers face when attempting to change their practices requires new ways of thinking about teacher learning and a willingness to move away from the simplistic 'deliver and apply' professional development that has been prominent in schools over the last forty years (Putnam and Borko, 1997; 2000).

Professional learning

A third form of teacher learning, 'professional learning', is not just about attending a one-off workshop, as in a professional development programme, or a sequence of courses or sessions, as in CPD. In contrast, it focuses on creating a learning environment in schools for teachers, including a framework or structure that incorporates multiple teacher learning processes to support change. Hence, professional learning is more about 'educating teachers' rather than 'training' them. In Hoban's words:

> A professional development program, therefore, is usually a one-off workshop or an isolated professional development day based on limited conditions and processes to support teacher learning – the presentation of new content over a relatively short time. In contrast, the design of a professional learning framework is long term and encapsulates multiple conditions or processes for teacher learning that interrelate as a system.
>
> (Hoban, 2002: 68)

In a school context, the structured teacher learning processes that support ongoing teacher learning can include reflection, discussion, action in classroom practice, new ideas or conceptual inputs, student feedback and working with colleagues on targeted workplace projects. Distinct from professional development and CPD, professional learning involves teachers taking responsibility for making decisions about the content or focus of their learning. Teacher learning processes are evident in all professional learning frameworks, but there may be different combinations. Encouraging their presence in a school context and how they interact will be more fully discussed in the chapter on 'The dynamics of action learning'.

As previously stated, the forms of teacher learning sometimes overlap; however, the major differences are summarised in Table 2.1.

Table 2.1 Forms of teacher learning

Forms of teacher learning	Features	Examples
Professional development /in-service	Short, one-off training events often delivered by 'experts' with teachers having little responsibility to determine content and no structured teacher learning processes back at school.	One-off school workshop, school development day or in-service.
Continuous professional development	Sequence of training events such as workshops, courses, programmes, conferences, often delivered by 'experts', with teachers having little responsibility to determine content and no structured teacher learning processes back in the school.	Accreditation courses or degree, sequence of workshops or conferences.
Professional learning	Long-term approach with teachers having a major influence in determining the content. This form is also accompanied by a framework with multiple teacher learning processes and conditions to sustain teacher learning back at school.	Action learning, action research, teacher research, project-based learning, problem-based learning.

Some of the key ideas about professional learning, especially involving reflection and community, were noted by Revans himself in describing action learning, but he rarely used explicit educational terms because this was not his field of expertise. In fact, many of Revans' ideas were based on his own common sense and a pragmatic approach to workplace learning. Revans (1982b) noted that professional learning is not about the presentation of information, as often demonstrated in training workshops, but is about the creation of a learning environment in the workplace, so that participants can learn about themselves with the help of others and seek answers to questions that are relevant to their needs.

The examples of professional learning shown in Table 2.1 – action learning, action research, teacher research, problem-based learning and project-based learning – are all examples of professional learning frameworks. Although they have many features in common, there are some key differences that are highlighted in the next section. Particular attention is given to distinguishing between action learning and action research, because they are commonly confused.

Comparing action learning and action research

Both action learning and action research are examples of professional learning frameworks that evolved in the 1940s from different disciplines. Action learning originated in business management literature produced in the mid 1940s by Revans and focused on small groups of coal-mine managers who met regularly to share experiences and seek solutions to their workplace problems. As noted by Revans, 'action learning, in simple English, becomes a social process; a lot of people start to learn with and from each other and a learning community comes into being' (Revans, 1982a: 69–70). He called the group of participants who meet regularly to share experiences and comment on each other's work-related issues or problems a 'set' that is at the 'cutting edge of every action learning programme' (1983a: 14). He also placed the highest importance on the honest sharing of experiences, whereby group discussions confirm or disconfirm personal reflections. This enables action plans to crystallise for each person. Revans (1982b) stated that personal honesty resulting in self-disclosure to colleagues was the most important feature of an action learning set or community. This disclosure establishes a trust that builds up over time between members of a set, enabling them to share more personal matters and discuss both their successes and failures in attempting to improve their practice.

Although Revans himself never gave a one-sentence definition of action learning, he was adamant that the social interaction among a small group is the key feature that is fundamental to action learning. Other authors have since provided their own definitions, as shown in the following three quotations from the business literature:

Action learning is a continuous process of learning and reflection, supported by colleagues, with an intention of getting things done. Through action learning individuals learn with and from each other by working on real problems and reflecting on their own experiences . . . We know that making powerful decisions is greatly enhanced by working with others. The focus, however, is essentially on the individual . . . The set enables this process to take place through concentrated group effort focused on the issues of each individual.

(McGill and Beaty, 1995: 21)

Action learning builds on the relationship between reflection and action. Learning by experience involves reflection, i.e. reconsidering past events, making sense of our actions, and possibly finding new ways of behaving at future events . . . Taking part in an action learning set provides the time and space to attend to the relationship, i.e. the link between reflection and learning. Set members enable their colleagues to understand, explore and judge their situation as well as helping to realise underlying feelings which influence behaviour.

(McGill and Brockbank, 2004: 13)

Action learning theory propounds that professionals will learn in the most effective way by focusing on actual organisational settings, within a supporting and challenging framework of enquiry, by peer group interaction and where personal empowerment can be encouraged through learner interdependency. It is about individuals learning from experience through reflection and action, usually to solve problems at work. This process, which is individually focused, uses a learning group, known as a 'set', which provides a forum wherein the set member's ideas can be challenged within a supportive environment.

(Gregory, 1994: 43)

For the purposes of this book, action learning in schools is defined as a professional learning framework involving a small group of teachers (four to eight is often recommended) who regularly reflect and share their experiences as a community to help them understand or address a school-related issue, dilemma, problem or project. The emphasis of action learning is on the social interaction between the teachers as they share their experiences and learn from each other. It should be noted that this is what teachers usually value the most when they engage in any form of teacher learning. Even when teachers attend a professional development programme in the form of an after-school workshop, it is commonly remarked that the most valuable part is often the unplanned sharing of stories with a colleague who teaches a similar subject or grade. Indeed, this sharing of experiences may not have anything to do with the goals of the workshop, but teachers resonate with others who experience similar challenges and issues. Action learning, therefore, highlights this important aspect, the sharing of anecdotal experiences and narratives with colleagues who work in, and understand, similar classroom contexts (Clandinin and Connelly, 1996).

A key issue highlighted by Pedler (2008) and Inglis (1994) is that action learning can have different goals or foci for the members. For example, a set may comprise people who have an individual focus, with each member working in their own setting and bringing their own individual issues and problems to the group for discussion. At the other extreme, a set may have a group focus, with a specified target or an organisational problem to solve. In this context, discussion in the group is focused on ways to find a solution to the common issue. Alternatively, a blend or hybrid of these approaches may be used. For example, a set may have a group focus, but there may be a variety of ways in which an individual can interpret and focus their own action learning efforts towards this group goal. In short, the outcome of action learning can be solving individual problems or shared group problems, or a combination of the two.

In contrast, action research originated in the social sciences and was first conceptualised by Kurt Lewin (1946) as a way for people in minority groups to become more aware of their situations and possible solutions. There are a variety of interpretations or emphases of action research and, like action learning, these may have a group or individual focus (Stenhouse, 1979). Here are three definitions of action research, as provided by key authors in the field:

Action research is a form of collective self-reflective enquiry undertaken by participants in the social situations in order to improve the rationality and justice of their own social or educational practices, as well as their understanding of these practices and the situations in which these practices are carried out. Groups of participants can be teachers, students, principals, parents and other community members, – any group with a shared concern. The approach is only action research when it is collaborative, though it is important to realise that the action research of the group is achieved through the critically examined action of individual group members . . . The linking of the terms 'action' and 'research' highlights the essential feature of the approach: trying out ideas in practice as a means of improvement and as a means of increasing knowledge about the curriculum, teaching and learning.

(Kemmis and McTaggart, 1988: 5)

Action research is any systematic inquiry conducted by teacher researchers, principals, school counsellors, or other stakeholders in the teaching/learning environment, to gather information about the ways that their particular schools operate, how they teach, and how well their students learn. This information is gathered with the goals of gaining insights, developing reflective practice, effecting positive changes in the school environment (and on educational practices in general), and improving student outcomes and the lives those involved.

(Mills, 2000: 6)

Action research is about taking action based on research and researching the action taken. Action research has been used in a variety of settings, including schools, hospitals, health clinics, community agencies, government units, and other environments. It can be used to enhance everyday work practices to resolve specific problems, and to develop special projects and programs. Action research in schools is also called practitioner research, teacher inquiry or teacher research . . . Good teachers engage in reflection, a key component of action research. But action research is more than reflection. It emphasises a systematic research approach that is cyclical in nature, alternating between action and reflection, continuously refining methods and interpretations based on understandings developed in earlier cycles.

(Ary *et al.*, 2006: 538–9)

In summary, while both action research and action learning involve cycles of reflection and action to learn from experience, the approaches have a different emphasis. The emphasis of action learning is on the social sharing of personal experiences among a small group, whereas the emphasis of action research is on systematic data collection that is made public. Although action research can be conducted individually or in groups (as in collaborative action research), action learning is always done in a group (usually of four to eight people), and discussions are normally guided by a facilitator. This is because the centrepiece of action learning is the team discussions whereby individuals share their personal reflections about a workplace issue or problem, with the expectation that group sharing will provide additional inputs. Based on these inputs, action plans devised to solve a workplace issue are implemented after the meetings and then discussed again at subsequent meetings in a recursive manner. This distinction between action learning and action research is well explained by McGill and Beaty:

> Action learning as a process is more general an approach to learning. Research is not the primary aim and the project may not involve any formal research at all. The individual is undertaking learning through the process of reflection in the set and therefore the process is essentially a group process. In action research, the researcher may be a lone individual, although there will inevitably be others involved in the project ... So while action learning may involve some research in the action phase, it is not essentially a research-oriented venture and indeed the research undertaken may use techniques quite different from those advocated by action research.
>
> (McGill and Beaty, 1995: 32)

Table 2.2 Comparison of action research and action learning

Feature	Action research	Action learning
Founder	Kurt Lewin (1946)	Reg Revans (1945)
Structure	Ongoing with cycles	Ongoing with cycles
Emphasis	'Research' through systematic data collection to answer a research question	'Learning' through team discussions of personal experiences
Learning Processes	Plan, action, implement, evaluate	Reflection, sharing, action, feedback
Participants	Individually or in a group	Always in a group of 4–8 people, with meetings every few weeks
Facilitator	Not usually	Usually

Similarly, Zuber-Skerritt (1993) maintains that action learning and action research are similar in that they have cycles of action and reflection, but action research is more rigorous because of its emphasis on research and because it is made public: 'the difference between action learning and action research is the same as that difference between learning and research' (Zuber-Skerritt, 1993: 46). The similarities and differences between action learning and action research are summarised in Table 2.2.

Evidence is used in both action learning and in action research; however, the evidence in action research is systematic and rigorous, whereas the evidence in action learning is often more informal, such as the sharing of anecdotal experiences.

The development of action learning in non-educational settings

After action learning was initially tried with mining managers in England in the mid 1940s, the next wave of implementation was in the 1950s in the palm oil plantations of Nigeria. Local forests provided thousands of jobs, with many different palm oil plantations and over a hundred small mills scattered around the city of Enugu. The problem was that many of these mills were not adequately profitable. So, instead of closing down, small numbers of managers were grouped together in action learning sets, as guided by the Institute of Management and Productivity at the University of N'suka. The outcome was that the plantation managers helped each other to become more profitable and thus saved the jobs of thousands of workers. Action learning was used in Nigeria as a strategy for workplace learning, especially for managers, and it then spread to Egypt, India and other countries (Revans, 1982b).

In the late 1960s, ten large hospitals in London were experiencing severe management difficulties. Not only were the hospitals operating beyond their budgets and the subject of many complaints from patients, but there was very low morale among management staff. Between 1965 and 1969, a systematic plan for managers was instigated, involving managers being placed in action learning sets. The result was that the hospital managers were learning about themselves and their colleagues as they collaboratively solved their workplace problems and issues. Over time, the hospitals became more efficient to run, morale improved, and fewer patient complaints were received. Other industries that have used action learning for the workplace learning of managers include the Victorian Public Service Board in Australia, engineers on the Siberian gas pipeline and executives in the General Electric Company (Keys, 1996). Fundamental to all of these efforts in using action learning is the bringing together of small groups of people who manage in similar areas to collaboratively solve their workplace problems and issues. According to Revans:

Such variations upon what must always remain the same simple idea – that those with responsible jobs to do, whether managers or not, learn best with and from each other when systematically brought together during the doing of those jobs – are, of course, bound to deepen our knowledge and understanding of this fundamental human drive.

(Revans, 1982b: 74)

Action learning continued to blossom in different workplace settings into the 1990s. It was used in a wide range of settings such as:

- executives in a textile company in Wales (Lewis, 1991);
- managers in a private hospital (Miller, 2003);
- supervisors in an electronic firm (Boddy, 1991);
- doctors in a hospital in England (Winkless, 1991);
- university students in a Diploma of Religious Education in England (Robinson, 2001);
- insurance agents attempting to improve the quality of their service in New Zealand (Schlesinger, 1991); and
- university students in health care education (Wade and Hammick, 1999).

To get an understanding of how action learning has been used to promote workplace learning in business contexts, two examples are explored in more detail.

Example 1: Action learning in the Williams Grand Prix racing team

In 1995, six foremen who worked for the Williams Grand Prix racing team participated in an action learning programme for six months to improve their practice in the workplace (Giles, 1997). This included improving ways to solve problems, handle discipline and build teams. Each of the foremen selected their own issue/problem and had regular meetings with the other members to assist each other to address their issues. There were four stages in the meetings to structure support for each individual: (i) listening to the individual relate their experiences and identify an issue; (ii) sharing perceptions among the group to gain different insights on the issue; (iii) identifying options to address the issue; and (iv) choosing the best option with an agreed action plan. The range of issues raised by individuals in the group, along with the action plans and outcomes, are outlined in Table 2.3.

Table 2.3 shows that each foreman identified a personal issue to investigate, which was discussed by the group to devise an action plan. Also, because of the structured interaction from the group or set, each of the action plans was different and specific to the person's need and context. However, it can be seen from the table that some of the action learning plans were more

Table 2.3 Personal issues raised by foremen in an action learning group at Williams Grand Prix Engineering

Personal Issue	What it became	Actions	Outcomes
Foreman A: Efficiency of running the 5-axis machine	A problem of coordinating operation of the machine among a group	Devised a trial way of coordinating team to operate the machine	Initial improvement but then communication problems arose again
Foreman B: Uncomfortable situation in being open and honest	A common problem of being confident about saying what you think	Collect examples Role play in group	More open communication – People became more assertive and supportive
Foreman C: Time management	An issue of responsibility and control	Define role Keep and analyse time log Confronting situations	Gaining in personal confidence and helping to define role
Foreman D: People management	Becoming more assertive and less aggressive, gaining cooperation	Learning and applying a more appropriate liaison style	Better control over priorities and learning people management skills
Foreman E: Feeling not consulted by management	Improving the foremen's meetings	Collecting views and liaising with the General Manager	Better meeting structure and feeling better personally
Foreman F: What am I responsible for?	Defining his role in the new plant, sorting sub-contract issues Delegation	Analysing a time log Reviewing the competence of the team Delegation	Changing personal style Delegating more Becoming less stressed

(Source: Adapted from Giles, 1997)

successful than others when implemented. Whereas there was no real improvement for foreman A, there was an improvement in work-related issues for the other five members of the set. It should be noted that there were fortnightly meetings over a six-month period, with plans devised at each meeting. The plans were implemented after each meeting and then discussed at the subsequent meeting (Giles, 1997).

Example 2: Action learning at MCB University Press

In 1994, a vision for the growth of MCB University Press in the UK had been formulated, and it was decided that ten members of the senior management team would engage in action learning to devise plans to implement the vision (Reid, 1994). Accordingly, a set of ten managers gathered together to devise ways to implement the strategic vision plan. A system of meetings was planned, such as a half-day and full-day meeting every month, to focus on the discussion of action plans and reflections, which there then interspersed with workshops on a needs basis. Some of the specific projects nominated were: benchmarking for quality; evaluation of MCB's copyright procedures; launching a region-specific journal; developing a qualitative framework for editorial excellence; developing a strategy for distribution handling and stockholding of publications and promotional materials; and implementing the key training requirements for the new sales operations department. The projects ran for eight months and culminated in each set member giving a written and oral presentation to the board of directors, who then gave them feedback on their efforts.

Conclusion

It is only in the last twenty years that action learning has been used in schools as an alternative to traditional, one-off professional development or in-service programmes. Although teacher learning can occur in these brief programmes, this type of learning usually reinforces existing practice rather than generates a change in practice. Because teaching is so complex, efforts to change something so multidimensional need to be accompanied by a professional learning framework, with embedded teacher learning processes and conducive conditions in schools. While other forms of teacher learning, such as one-off workshops promoted by professional development, and sequences of courses promoted by continuous professional development, can involve teacher learning processes, their existence in the workplace is often ad hoc and inconsistent.

We know that action learning 'works' because it has been successfully used in business contexts for over seventy years. In our rapidly changing educational landscape, the timing is right to incorporate action learning in schools. However, the educational processes underpinning action learning have not been well articulated in business literature because the writers did not have an educational 'language' to fully explain the processes and conditions necessary for change. This book provides such a 'language', as well as examples of action learning conducted mostly in Australian school contexts over the last ten years. The next chapter explains some of the conditions and processes that enable action learning to occur.

Chapter 3

Enabling action learning: getting started

with Stephen Dinham[1]

Introduction and overview

> If a change is to be effective and lasting, it is necessary to change what people know, think and can do, as it is people who make change happen.
>
> (paraphrasing Dinham, 2007a: 273)

As discussed earlier in 'Positioning action learning', no school-based reform operates in a vacuum. External factors, including socio-political contexts, are always extremely important in informing what happens within any individual school. Schools and school systems are constantly under pressure from national and regional governments to bring about improved student learning outcomes. There are frequent assertions from governments, policymakers, business communities and the media that students are not learning effectively or that standards in literacy or numeracy have fallen (e.g. Donnelly, 2007). Thus external factors will, directly or indirectly, play an important role in the change process in school communities.

Centralised policies intended to ensure that schools and teachers are accountable for ever-improving student learning outcomes are frequently being revised and developed in many western education systems. Consider, for example, the national curriculum experience over the last two decades in England, the *No Child Left Behind* programme in the United States and the current movements towards a national curriculum in Australia. At the same time there has been movement over the last decade to decentralise the day-to-day management of schools. As Caldwell and Spinks comment:

> There is thus the paradox of simultaneous centralisation and decentralisation. An issue has been the linkage between these frameworks

1 Research Director, Teaching, Learning and Leadership, Australian Council for Educational Research.

and capacities at school level that come with self-management on the one hand, and learning outcomes for students on the other.

(Caldwell and Spinks, 1998: 10–11)

Ever-increasing political, system and media influences have led demands for schools to perform. This in turn has increased pressure on school principals to provide more extensive professional development programmes for staff. Meeting these demands involves applying for additional funding sources to enable these programmes to be sustained; ensuring school policies and practices align with state and commonwealth standards; and interpreting test results to inform school improvement.

In this paradoxical climate, action learning has gained momentum in schools, as it has been viewed as an important professional learning process, enabling teachers to:

- manage their own professional learning agenda collaboratively;
- respond to the needs of their students in their own school context;
- set up processes that can provide constructive feedback about teaching practices;
- embed time in school timetables to experiment with new ideas and strategies; and
- ensure that time is also provided for teachers to reflect both individually and as action learning teams on their ideas and implementation strategies.

Action learning teams[2] are often formed by bringing together staff from different parts and levels of an organisation in the manner of a jigsaw. Contemporary organisations are frequently fragmented, owing to functionalism and specialisation, and can be loosely coupled. This results in individuals and groups within organisations being largely unaware of, or even in competition with, each other. Bringing together members of an organisation into an action learning team can help to reduce this fragmentation and identify patterns that may otherwise be missed, therefore increasing efficiency and production.

With action learning, team members' knowledge and expertise are recognised, complemented, expanded and deepened. They learn from each other and sometimes from others outside the organisation, prior to and in the course of dealing with a particular issue. It is a hands-on learning experience consistent with adult learning and constructivist practices. Teamwork and leadership skills are developed, and members gain a greater understanding of the total organisation and how their work integrates into this whole (Dinham *et al.*, 2008). This helps people 'make sense' of their

---

2 The term action learning team, rather than set, is generally used in this discussion.

work, the work of others and the overall work of the organisation. This in turn improves social as well as technical processes within the organisation (Weinstein, 1998: 151).

In our experience, action learning encourages empowerment and 'taking charge', rather than reacting to external demands and forces; 'thinking outside the square'; and novel solutions to what may have been regarded as intractable problems. In common with action-research, members work collaboratively to remove obstacles that are preventing greater organisational efficiency and productivity (Kemmis and McTaggart, 2005: 561). The learning that occurs as a result of a particular action learning project then becomes a foundation and resource for subsequent issues. In this way, individual and team learning informs and enables organisational learning and the development of a learning community that is more adept at coping with change (Senge *et al.*, 2000; Dinham, 2007b; Weinstein, 1998: 151).

It is important to recognise that action learning is not a linear, fixed, formulaic process. The discussions may dwell on certain issues for several meetings or be suspended while other more important things are happening in the school. The important point is that the team is aware that the regular pattern of reflection on experiences and sharing insights with other team members needs to continue wherever possible. To make the most of the process, it is important that context and organisational history are considered, and the particular approach adopted needs to fit both the context and purpose. This also means that adaptation and flexibility are required from all team members.

Zuber-Skerritt (2002: 147), in referring to both action learning and action research, summarises some aspects that contribute to team success:

- *Success/worth* – an action learning team that suggests tangible solutions and success through the process can enhance both an individual's and a group's self-worth.
- *Fun/enjoyment* – although teams work hard, and often in their own time, as members experience a collegiate spirit and have a shared goal, they often have fun as well.
- *Freedom/choice* – team members are often able to choose to be involved, and action learning encourages creativity and innovation throughout, especially when participants have the freedom and choice to explore alternative solutions.
- *Belonging/respect/love* – as team members are united by shared goals and work in close proximity to each other, over time they can develop and share a common language and culture. Through this process, they usually come to respect and like, or at least appreciate, each other.

Action learning should not be confused with more formal strategies and approaches, such as cross-functional work teams, committees and matrix structures (Dixon, 1998: 44). Action learning teams are more organic, flexible, dynamic and focused, with a known 'shelf-life', usually in the range of six months to three years (McGill and Beaty, 2001: 19), as opposed to committees and other structures, which may address a wider range of issues and can go on operating indefinitely.

We will now consider some of the following features of action learning in more detail, particularly those aspects associated with how it can be enabled in school contexts:

- selecting, defining and focusing the issue, dilemma or problem;
- school leadership;
- team formation and membership;
- leadership of the action learning team;
- know your people;
- collaboration and professional dialogue;
- the external facilitator;
- goal setting: targets and timelines;
- how action learning teams work; and
- implementation and 'take off'.

Selecting, defining and focusing the issue, dilemma or problem

Action learning is not an esoteric exercise. Action learning targets real issues of significance to participants, the organisation and its clients. Therefore, the selection and delineation of the subject or focus for a particular action learning process is of great importance. Some recent school-based issues, dilemmas and problems that have been tackled include:

- improving the senior literacy levels of a newly established collegiate school where the student population were largely the first of their families to continue with post compulsory education;
- addressing higher-order thinking and problem-solving skills in primary mathematics;
- investigating the engagement of boys in middle school, especially in the area of literacy;
- improving the study skills of year seven and eight secondary students; and
- increasing involvement of the parent community in the culture of a school.

There are a number of approaches to the selection of a problem or focus around which professional learning and research will take place. Some advocate forming a team prior to selecting a problem (see Bierema, 1998: 98), with the team then determining the area or issue for study. Others suggest selecting a problem and then forming a team suited to addressing this task. In some cases, both approaches are undertaken iteratively, with leaders often playing important initiating and mediating roles as a project and action learning team formalise. The action learning may have an external or internal impetus. For example, a group of principals might arrange to meet every two weeks to share the particular dilemmas and issues in their particular schools. Each principal would then give advice or suggestions according to the issue raised. Alternatively, the stage two teachers in a primary school may initiate an action learning process to corporately improve the focus on science. A school may apply for a project funded by a system, using action learning processes to improve the district's performance in the national literacy tests.

A second example in a school district may be a directive to examine what factors are inhibiting retention at the level of senior school. The pressure can also come from outside the organisation, through, for example, government funding, changes in marketplace conditions or socio-economic change.

In reality, action learning occurs within the context of two overlapping and interacting environments: the external environment within which the organisation is situated and operates, and the internal environment of the organisation. Each environment is under continual pressure for change and each influences the other, according to Kember (2000: 59).

Another area where the literature is ambivalent is the issue of the primary audience and purpose for action learning. Are the potential benefits primarily for the members of the team, or the organisation as a whole, or a mixture of both? McGill and Beaty (2001: 16–17) see the primary audience as team members, with possible positive implications for the organisation. Something the literature is clear about is the importance of having support from the 'top'. Action learning processes that have the support of leaders have a greater likelihood of success. Leaders can provide resources, advice and encouragement, as well as helping to neutralise opposition and 'smooth the way' (Weinstein, 1998: 154).

Another important criterion in the case of education is whether the issue or problem 'involves a matter on which student or teacher performance could and should be improved' (Sagor, 2000: 47). Ideally, action learning in school contexts should relate directly to the 'core business' of schooling, and should be consistent and congruent with a school's management plan and other key strategic documents and policies. It is often possible to demonstrate how the completion of the action learning cycle complements and adds value to these policies and plans, to the work of the school and to its core business: teacher quality and student accomplishment.

Our experience with action learning suggests there can be potential danger with beginning in an overly ambitious manner. In short, our research suggests that starting with a small focus is often more desirable, because being able to achieve something provides a positive beginning. For example, it may be preferable to concentrate the issue around a school year or stage, subject area or group of students, rather than involve the entire school. Given success, the action learning framework can then be applied to new areas, involving more staff and students. Starting with a large focus at the beginning can sometimes lead to a sense of failure if this becomes difficult to achieve. Besides, projects always seem to grow!

In selecting an area for action learning, it is important to proceed on a firm evidence base. To determine whether an area is suitable, the following questions are useful:

- Do we have a problem or issue in this area?
- What is the most personal and relevant issue we need to address?
- What are the indicators and manifestations of the problem?
- What are the trend data telling us? Is the problem becoming wider, deeper?
- How does the problem relate to other problems? What are the causes/ effects?
- What has been tried previously? What can be learned from this?
- What resources will we need?

In education, a common focus is ultimately the improvement of student achievement. This requires very careful consideration of the following important issues:

- what our assumptions about student learning are in this context;
- how student achievement will be defined and measured in valid and reliable ways;
- whether the timeframe for the project is sufficient to see a real impact; and
- the existence of other factors and initiatives that might also be influencing student achievement in this context.

Hawthorne or halo effects are common in educational change, and success of interventions can be overestimated, particularly in the absence of evidence of student performance over time.

School leadership

School education often operates in a hierarchical system of administration and management. Yet action learning requires a flat leadership structure, where collaborative leadership is embraced as members of the group take collective responsibility and exhibit shared leadership:

Action learning is a method of decision-making based on enhanced experiential learning. The core processes of experiential learning and creative problem-solving are enhanced by the acquisition of additional relevant knowledge and the support of a co-learner group. Decisions are made, not by the group, but by the person owning the problem situation. The group is there to enhance their learning and decision-making process. Group members support each other by sharing the uncertainties of problem situations, by adding information from their own experience and resources, and by asking useful and challenging questions.

(Cusins, 1996: 26)

Action learning, because of its very nature, is more likely to begin in school environments where there is a desire for shared leadership. Therefore, the pervading model of leadership in the school, and particularly within the executive, plays an important role in encouraging or inhibiting action learning. It is perhaps unsurprising that the rise of action learning in school settings has coincided with the reframing of educational leadership to stress the importance and potential of distributed leadership.

Although the concept of distributed leadership can be traced back to social psychology in the 1950s, it is only in the last decade or so that the concept has achieved widespread prominence (Gronn, 2002). This prominence has coincided with changes in how educational leadership is conceptualised and enacted to reflect a number of realities: that teaching and learning, rather than management, should be the prime focus of the school; that principals cannot bear all the burden of school management and leadership owing to increasing pressures and demands being placed upon them and their schools; and that the contribution of distributed leadership to school functioning and student achievement has tended to be overlooked or undervalued (Spillane *et al.*, 2001; Gronn, 2002: 654).

Gronn (2002: 654–60) has considered the multiple meanings of distributed leadership, all of which fundamentally fall into two groups. The first sees distributed leadership as essentially additive (with more leaders and shared leadership), while the second, more holistic, approach includes forms of collaboration and participation based on trust and empowerment. Rather than spreading existing leadership and leadership responsibility across more people, a holistic view of distributed leadership is concerned with the synergies that can occur when people come together to work, plan, learn and act. This generates further leadership capacity within the individual and the organisation, leading to greater organisational effectiveness.

In many schools, typically it is the principal who gives expression to the type of leadership that permeates the school. The extent to which a school principal and their executive promote (holistic) distributed leadership can have a bearing on the potential success of action learning. The case study report for one high school noted:

The Principal of the secondary school said she was 'involved in all stages although [the project leader/deputy principal] was the driver . . . Distributed leadership was enhanced through the project, which had spread leadership across faculties . . . staff are taking on leadership roles'.

(Unpublished case study, Macropod High School)

Action learning thus sits comfortably with a holistic view of distributed school leadership, where there is growing recognition that school leaders have a key role in unlocking the unreleased and unrealised potential residing among teachers in educational organisations (Crowther *et al.*, 2002; York-Barr and Duke, 2004). In promoting such a leadership framework, the principal can play an important role in enabling action learning and enhancing the innovative capacity of the individual and the organisation.

Team formation and membership

It is crucially important to select the right mix of people for effective action learning to take place. Teams that are too small (less than four) or too large (more than eight) can have problems. How the team is constructed will depend on the focus issue or problem. It can be useful if team members are drawn from various areas of the school, to provide both a critical mass and diversity of views, experience and skill sets. A secondary desirable outcome of action learning is greater awareness, appreciation, cooperation and cohesion, which can arise from bringing together people from different stages or faculties. People may come and go over the course of an action learning cycle. Obviously, the longer the timeframe, the greater the likelihood that people will move roles or schools. Sometimes, the team doesn't become effective until someone leaves and the dynamics change (Aubusson *et al.*, 2006). Additionally, the action learning project could reach a stage where a new challenge or issue arises that requires additional staff expertise.

Most writers on action learning advocate that action learning team membership should be voluntary (see McGill and Beaty, 2001: 22). This can have the effect of engendering greater commitment. Teachers in schools tend to be overstretched, with little discretionary time. Forcing them to become part of an action learning team can be unwise, as it may lead to 'lip service' involvement and resentment of the project. However, there is a valid argument for judiciously selecting, or at the least encouraging, certain staff members to take part in an action learning team. Ideally, members should be invited on the basis of what they can add to the action learning process and what they can gain through such involvement.

Leadership of the action learning team

As we have seen, leadership should not be vertical in an action learning team. It should be characterised by sharing, collaboration and participation.

An earlier focus on the more technical aspects of educational administration and later management has turned more to leadership for enhancing teaching and learning. Sometimes the team leader is a member of the school executive, and, in other cases, the leader is a classroom teacher. Joint leadership is also possible because, in reality, most action learning teams should work in a highly collaborative manner as they learn and plan together. Dinham *et al.* (2008) refer to data from seven case studies of action learning in schools. This section draws on these data to discuss matters of leadership in school-based action learning. The experience of one primary school action learning team was described thus:

> Initially some members of the group were fearful of the workload and were concerned that the executive members of the group might act as 'supervisors.' Even though the eight members included four members of the school executive, the group did not have a 'supervisory' feel. All group members found the whole experience non-threatening.
>
> (Dinham *et al.*, 2008)

A secondary school action learning team commented that:

> The support from school leaders for the project, especially the Principal and project coordinator, was seen as essential. The project leader was described [by staff] as: 'constantly actively involved' and 'a big lynch pin but knew how to distribute leadership'.
>
> (Dinham *et al.*, 2008)

Principals had significant influence over the composition of project teams, including having the final say on leadership and membership, without directing teachers to take part. However, in several cases, principals confided to the researchers how they had induced influential, potentially negative or obstructive teachers to be part of the teams (see Dinham *et al.*, 2008); for example:

> Some teachers were invited onto the team to provide an opportunity for building leadership expertise rather than because of a special commitment to the project or perceived leadership qualities. In this way, it was hoped [by the co-leaders] that the Quality Teaching/Action Learning (QTAL) project could contribute to building long-term leadership capacity of the school. In this distributed leadership model, each member of the QTAL leadership team would plan the project's progress determining what actions to take, what evidence to collect and analysing this evidence to determine further actions.

Project teams spent time, prior to and in the early stages of the project, meeting and planning to formulate the goals for their individual projects.

These conversations were important in framing and directing projects. However, things did not always run smoothly, as the same primary school report noted:

> Members of the QTAL leadership team confided that at least two members of the initial project team were reluctant members and did not develop the enthusiasm or leadership qualities needed to promote and lead the project within their stage [grade/year] groups. However, both left the school during the project and their replacements in the leadership group proved more productive.
>
> (Dinham et al., 2008)

Team leaders in some action learning projects developed a higher profile within and, in many cases, outside their schools than they had previously. They worked with members of the project team drawn from across the school and, in some cases, with teachers engaged with the project from other schools. The case study report for a primary school noted the importance of committed leadership from the project leader: 'The ICT teacher [Information Communication Technology project leader] "knew where the school needed to go; she was really committed to it". She was described by a team member as "our guiding light"'.

In citing conditions for the success of a project at another primary school, the evaluation team found as major factors:

> [The] Leadership of the two assistant principals who had experienced similar projects, were confident, well respected and 'had clout' with both staff and the executive . . . [There was also a] strong sense of commitment, shared responsibility and mutual support initially between the two executive leaders, which later developed more widely among the majority of the leadership group.
>
> (Dinham et al., 2008)

In interviews at the case study schools, principals recounted how they had selected project leaders both on the basis of their leadership skills, and on their potential for leadership.

Overall, it was apparent that project leaders had grown into the role, gaining leadership skills, experience, confidence and status. It was also apparent that members of project teams grew in their leadership capacity during the course of projects, particularly those not in formal leadership positions. Less experienced teachers who were team members often grew most in confidence, and some seemed to enjoy the influence and profile they gained through project membership. Clearly, the project leaders, with support from their principals, led their teams well, with collaboration and teamwork being essential factors in the success of the projects and in connecting the projects with their colleagues in the rest of the school.

Know your people

School leaders interested in facilitating action learning teams need to have a sound knowledge and understanding of the various staff members who might take part. As noted, they may need to engage in a degree of talent spotting, coaching and encouragement to get the right mix of team membership. A certain degree of creative tension or dissonance within the team is not a bad thing if it causes people to question their preconceptions and practices.

Dinham (2008) has identified three key broad groups of people who need to be considered when change is being contemplated and therefore when setting up an action learning project.

1   *The enthusiasts* – supporters of the change who will be prepared to commit time and effort to the initiative. These people can range from the informed and 'hard-headed' enthusiasts to the naive. Enthusiasts may have experience and expertise in the area, or may be prepared to 'give it a go' if such familiarity is lacking. They tend to be early adopters and risk takers, although they sometimes let their heart rule their head. There are two subgroups of enthusiasts: those who will cheerfully support almost anything, and those who will provide support for a particular issue. Enthusiasts are also initiators of change.

2   *The watchers* – as the name implies, these people are generally compliant, calculative and open to persuasion. Watchers are prepared to consider a change on its merits and can go either way on an issue. As with enthusiasts, they will go along with a leader who has won their respect and trust, suspending judgement until later. Over time, watchers can become increasingly involved and supportive if they are exposed to convincing evidence and argument. Small successes can bring watchers onside. However, if the change process is handled badly, watchers can withdraw their support and involvement.

3   *The blockers* – these people may be opposed to a particular change, or change in general. They can be either active or passive in their opposition. Blockers will not be swayed by rational argument or evidence and can be counted on to resist change. Even if their opposition is muted, members of this kind may use their influence with others to obstruct and 'white-ant' the change. Alternatively, they may say little but will studiously ignore the change, waiting for it, and you, to go away. Blockers may have been in the school or system for some time, with their views having hardened over the years. 'Balkanisation' and 'group-think' can govern the thinking and actions of blockers.

As an educational leader, it is instructive to reflect on the numbers of each group for any proposed change. Knowledge of the organisation's history, culture and group dynamics is also important. Past failed attempts at change need to be understood and considered, as some blockers act as 'keepers of the nightmare'. They might say 'we tried that in 1975 and it didn't work'; it '. . . was a disaster', and so forth. Of course, blockers usually ignore their own role in such failures.

Schools and other educational institutions are not democracies however, and leaders have to make unpopular decisions at times for the overall betterment of the organisation. Additionally, much change is mandated, and the real issue is how to accommodate change of this nature and use it to the organisation's advantage. When it comes to decision-making, the most effective educational leaders possess both courage and strategic thinking (Dinham, 2007c).

Recent evaluations of the Australian Government Quality Teaching Programme (AGQTP) in New South Wales (NSW) schools highlighted the importance of leaders carefully considering the composition and influence of groups (Ewing et al., 2004, 2005; Aubusson et al., 2006). In forming these action learning teams in their schools, many principals thoughtfully and strategically selected project team leaders and encouraged team membership. In several cases, principals admitted to having induced key watchers and potential blockers to join project teams, operating on the 'Lyndon B. Johnson' theory that it would be better to have these people 'inside the tent' than outside. These principals reasoned that, once these people had become involved and had a personal stake in the projects, they would influence others to provide support or at least give the projects 'a go'.

In another research project that examined leadership for exceptional educational outcomes in junior secondary education, some principals of successful schools had made the decision to bypass the blockers altogether. They concentrated on encouraging and providing professional learning opportunities for groups of enthusiasts and watchers, hoping to achieve contagious effects from successful change across the wider school. There is a danger in this, in that the leader can be accused of 'playing favourites', but these principals realised that if one 'waits for everyone to get on the bus, it never leaves' (Dinham, 2005, 2007c).

A key aspect in all of this is knowing one's fellow staff – and, where relevant, community members – and how each might react to any change in the status quo. Over time, successfully managed change (and retirements and transfers) can see the weakening of the blockers' power base and the overcoming of a culture of negativity and resistance (Dinham, 2007a).

Collaboration and professional dialogue

Increased collaboration and communication among teachers are often reported outcomes of action learning. Team members often comment that shared 'deep' professional dialogue regarding teaching, has replaced the previous 'shallow' discussion about lesson content or student behaviour. Comments below illustrate the positive nature of dialogue:

> What worked was the real teamwork and collaboration within the executive and between staff members that has generated professional discussion and the ability to try new ways of doing things [high school]. Faculties were seen to be talking more and working more closely together: 'Staff resistant to change are now getting up and sharing'. A dialogue about teaching and learning has developed and people from different faculties are now talking and sharing, whereas they were 'their own cells in the past'. There is more understanding of secondary strategies in stage 3 [primary grades 5–6] and of primary strategies in stage 4 [secondary grades 7–8] [high school and several primary schools].
>
> (Dinham *et al.*, 2008)

The case study report for a high school noted that an outcome of successful team building was:

> Extensive teacher learning and teacher growth in risk taking and in confidence. Teachers who felt very hesitant about ICT in the classroom have developed new programs, which they are trialing, incorporating ICT and QT principles . . . These teachers have learnt new skills with the technology, and are using a greater range of resources.
>
> (Dinham *et al.*, 2008)

Action learning, team building and distributed leadership can provide a foundation for change. The case study report for another high school stated:

> The view was that there is 'a critical mass now, momentum'. A teacher stated it was 'a highlight of my career . . . so positive . . . I have learnt so much'. Teachers were 'enthusiastic, everyone likes it because it worked . . . agreed to do it, really enjoyed it, understood it, feel confident, even people teaching for years . . . feedback, reaffirmation, reassurance . . . re-enthused some teachers.'
>
> (Dinham *et al.*, 2008)

These comments all show the positive effect that action learning can have on a school community.

The external facilitator

Initially, Revans (1983a, b) did not advocate for the use of an external facilitator in action learning. He saw such a person as having the potential to dominate the process. The literature on organisational change and organisational development, however, suggests that it is very difficult to change an organisation wholly from within. More recently, therefore, many action learning theorists have discussed the importance of a 'set advisor'. In schools, this role has often been played by an academic partner or external facilitator.

The literature generally recommends the facilitator take a largely 'hands off, advisory role', where team members are driving the action learning project. They are able to call upon the external advisor where necessary, to be more a critical, informed friend than a judgemental expert. The role of the external adviser is considered in more detail in the chapter 'Facilitating action learning: The academic partner's role'.

Goal setting: Targets and timelines

Action learning targets or goals need to be both aspirational, in that high expectations are involved, and realistically capable of being 'hit'. Writing in respect of action research, Sagor comments:

> Choosing a focus for teacher research is a necessary, but not sufficient, first step. This is because choosing a target and seeing that target clearly can be two very different things. Generally the focus . . . pertains to student achievement . . . in other cases, the research focus relates to a teaching technique.
>
> (Sagor, 2000: 52–3)

Whatever the issue being studied, it is always worthwhile to spend some time clarifying the targets or desired outcomes before proceeding. If we are going to cite a target, it is important to state precisely and unambiguously exactly what it is we wish to accomplish.

In some cases, goals may initially be too narrow and may need to be broadened as action learning projects unfold. In other cases, goals can be too broad, and a narrowing of focus is required. Action learning teams can modify their goals as the process evolves, and in this way goals become more realistic and achievable. It would appear to be a mistake to adhere too closely to original timelines and goals. As action learning teams progress in their learning and intervention, they are increasingly in a better position to realistically appraise and modify, as necessary, their initial goals. To facilitate goal flexibility and adjustment, it is necessary to periodically measure and reflect on progress to date. Targets and indicators play an important role in this process. Without targets and evidence of the progress of the intervention, it may be tempting to proceed regardless, or to make faulty assumptions and decisions about the success, or otherwise, of the process.

It is also advantageous to stage or schedule key goal milestones. Unfocused, large ideas can prove daunting. Having some shorter-term, smaller goals and hitting attainable targets more regularly engender greater confidence and momentum. As well as teams being clear in their goals and plans, it is necessary to have a communication strategy for the rest of the organisation, to overcome misconceptions and to share successes with other staff members and wider stakeholders. In this way, support for action learning as a professional learning framework can be built and doubters won over.

How action learning teams work

There are a number of different models or approaches to the operation of action learning teams. At one end of the spectrum, teams are highly structured, with regular time cycles for meetings and allocated times for each participant to speak about their issue or problem. McGill and Beaty (2001: 29–37) suggest that

> three hours is very tight for a set meeting with over five people. A good rule of thumb is that an allocation of half an hour per set member plus half an hour of opening and closing is a minimum below which the depth of said work would be seriously impaired.

However, such a time allocation is unrealistic for teachers in school-day settings. While such meetings still need to have a purpose and structure, they are likely to be briefer, more dynamic and free-form than those in the corporate sector. McGill and Beaty (2001) do make some important suggestions, including the need for meetings to take place in an appropriate setting that is free from noise and interruptions, the need to set the scene in meetings to ensure people are comfortable and not tired, the need for ground rules and the importance of breaks for relaxation and re-energising.

McGill and Beaty (2001: 36) suggest a number of ground rules including:

- confidentiality and trust;
- active listening;
- respect for serious conversations;
- regular attendance;
- flexibility; and
- time for reflection and strategic questioning.

McGill and Beaty (2001: 37–44) also stress the importance of team members getting to know each other; agreeing on the content and purpose of each team meeting; equitably allocating time to individuals; using time effectively; recording the actions and follow-up required from meetings; and the need for team members to be self-critical and reflective. It is important that every member comes prepared for each team meeting and follows up on agreed actions. Without such cooperation, input and commitment, too much of the burden falls upon too few members of the action learning team, potentially resulting in frustration.

Meetings themselves should be kept as free of extraneous factors as possible, so that members can maximise time and attention on the matter at hand. It is a good idea for all team members to have access to the agenda, if there is one, and for materials to be distributed several days before the meeting. Duties such as chairing the meeting and writing up minutes can be rotated around team members. Keeping to time is essential, as time is precious to teachers. It may be necessary in some instances to remind non-compliant, difficult or dysfunctional team members of their obligations, or even to offer them the chance to withdraw from the team.

There is something to be said for conducting meetings 'off-site', so that team members can give the agenda and matters for discussion their undivided attention, free from interruptions and the temptation to leave the meeting to deal with an unrelated issue. In the case of schools, releasing teachers from some of their duties to attend planning meetings is advantageous to project success.

Implementation and 'take off'

An important issue in action learning is knowing when enough learning and planning have occurred to enable the action or intervention to begin. The quality of the implementation is as important as the quality of the plan to the overall success of an action learning project. Lanahan and Maldonado (1998) describe the implementation of an action learning project as '. . . the make-or-break stage of the process. The most brilliant solutions developed by the most capable groups can fail to achieve their potential if the implementation lacks drive' (Lanahan and Maldonado, 1998: 83). They also suggest that 'the following factors are vital to successful implementation:

- the champions must carefully monitor the progress of the implementation team;
- the checkpoint meetings must occur on schedule; and
- obstacles to implementation must be identified, addressed, and resolved' (Lanahan and Maldonado, 1998: 83).

Challenges to getting started

Based on their research, Bourner and Frost (1996) note the importance of feelings and emotions as well as strategy in getting started on action learning projects:

It starts with nervousness and anxiety combined with either excitement or scepticism at the outset. Suggestions that it is likely to involve a degree of personal and/or professional disclosure seem to heighten the level of anxiety experienced at this stage. As the set meetings get under way this, typically, is replaced by enthusiasm for the process mixed with some surprise that it is an enjoyable experience (which is sometimes contrasted with other experiences of learning). By the time that the program finishes there is often a desire to keep the action learning set running on an unfacilitated or self-facilitated basis.

(Bourner and Frost, 1996: 17)

A key aspect in 'getting going' relates to goal setting and planning. It is essential that team members and, where relevant, team advisers develop an agreement as to what the team is hoping to achieve and the means by which they will do so. However, it is by no means essential that this be determined a priori. The first step is to agree to meet and then to resolve and define issues and problems to be addressed through the action learning process. As a general rule, it is better to start than to procrastinate. Teams often fear a false start, making a mistake and its consequences, in particular for their students, if they get it wrong. But action learning is an iterative process in which mistakes are inevitable. Nevertheless, it is important to avoid harm and to learn from mistakes that will occur whenever significant innovation is sought. One way to reduce the impact of mistakes and to initiate action early is by 'starting small'. With this approach, goals need to be both pertinent and achievable. It is acceptable and even desirable to modify goals and change the focus of the action learning project once team members have learned more about the area under consideration. As team members gain confidence, team effectiveness grows and greater knowledge and skills are acquired, members will be in a better position to direct and modify the project as needed.

Another key factor in the implementation and progress of action learning teams is the level of the engagement and commitment of team members. Aubusson *et al.* (2006: 24–5) commented:

In general, a feature common among schools that were deemed less successful . . . was a lack of engagement with Quality Teaching and action learning and this reflected a seeming lack of commitment by the project teams or staff involved. The problem for some project teams appeared to be not that action learning is incompatible with writing a unit or integrating ICT, but that these content-based or product-based initiatives distracted them from a focus on pedagogy and action learning, redirecting them to an often mechanistic designing of a programme of work. It was only in later stages of report writing that the importance of action learning and the Quality Teaching Model assumed importance.

Marquardt (1999: 13) identified seven factors that can militate against successful action learning:

1   inappropriate choice of issue or problem;
2   lack of support from top management;
3   lack of time;
4   poor mix of participants;
5   lack of commitment by participants;
6   all action and no learning;
7   incompetent set adviser.

Each of the above can result from failure to consider and adhere to the basic principles for effective action learning outlined earlier in this chapter. However, even given such problems, Marquardt (2004) sees much evidence for the 'marvellous power and value of action learning':

> Action learning works not because of luck, but because it inherently interweaves a wide array of organisational, psychological, sociological, and educational theories and principles – as well as key elements of ethics, political science, engineering, and systems thinking. Each of the components reinforces and leverages the power of action learning. The simplicity and immediate applicability of action learning have enabled organisations around the world to achieve success in problem-solving, team building, organisational learning, and leadership development.
>
> (Marquardt, 2004: 32)

Conclusion

Action learning does not occur spontaneously. It needs a good deal of planning and decision-making in many different areas. This chapter has outlined some of the principles and practicalities of enabling and beginning the action learning process in a school. We have seen that action learning is focused on real issues and problems and on finding and enacting solutions to change what people know, think and can do. These issues can be related to a personal need of each individual, the group as a whole or a project chosen to improve the school in general. In addition to selecting the focus of the action learning, there are many other considerations, such as leadership in the school and leadership of the team; getting an appropriate cross-section of people; knowing how to run action learning meetings; allocating time and resources for team meetings; accessing a facilitator; developing a culture of collaboration and professional dialogue; and communicating outcomes to others in the school. The next chapter examines the dynamics of action learning, analysing the interactions among reflection, community, action and feedback.

Chapter 4

The dynamics of action learning

Although the characteristics of action learning were originally explained by Revans over twenty years ago (1982b, 1983b), the educational processes underpinning action learning have not been well articulated. This is because the original writers in the business literature did not have educational backgrounds and, hence, did not have a 'language' to clearly articulate the processes underpinning action learning. One author, however, in business literature did attempt to explain these multiple influences. Cusins (1995) viewed the process of action learning as the interaction of four sources or types of learning: (i) experiential learning; (ii) creative problem solving; (iii) acquisition of relevant knowledge; and (iv) co-learner group support. These four types of learning were represented by Cusins as a linear cycle involving an event or activity, reflective observation, planning and application. Importantly, he noted that it is the combined influence of these four types of learning that result in the ongoing synergistic change that is characteristic of action learning.

In educational terms, action learning is underpinned by four main teacher learning processes – reflection, community, action and feedback – which interrelate and enhance each other when operating effectively. In essence, a synergy is created by these four learning processes interacting to create powerful influences that can lead to a change in teaching practice. A synergy occurs when the sum of the 'parts' or 'processes' is greater than considering each one separately. In short, reflection supports personal thinking to contribute to group discussions, which enhances action plans and feedback from colleagues or students and so on. Hence, it is the combination of the four learning processes that is important to initiate and sustain teacher learning. In addition to the four key learning processes, there are also several 'workplace conditions' needed for action learning to flourish. These include principal approval, a collegial work culture and leadership within the group or 'set'. These conditions will be more fully explained in the chapter 'Sustaining professional learning'.

The professional learning literature is permeated with examples of studies of how teachers can learn from each of these teacher learning processes. For example, there are numerous studies in which teachers learn by reflecting on their experiences (Baird, 1992; Dewey, 1933; Hatton and Smith, 1995; LaBoskey, 1994; Loughran, 1995; Russell and Bullock, 1999); by developing as a community and sharing ideas (Day, 1999; Grossman and Wineburg, 2000; Wenger, 1998); by experimenting with practice and putting ideas into action (Kolb, 1984; Mills, 2000); and by seeking feedback from students or colleagues on efforts for change (Hoban, 2004). However, what is not well articulated in the literature is how a professional learning framework, such as action learning, integrates these four teacher learning processes and how they work together dynamically to sustain workplace learning in schools (Hoban et al., 2005). The aim of this chapter, therefore, is to further explain the four main teacher learning processes that underpin action learning and to demonstrate how they work together synergistically to sustain action learning. This will be illustrated with examples of two action learning projects in Australia, one from a primary school and one from a high school.

Teacher learning processes underpinning action learning

Teacher learning process 1: Reflection

The first process, reflection, involves participants rethinking about something problematic to make sense of their experiences, to help them to cope with similar situations in the future. Initially proposed by Dewey (1933) as a particular form of thinking, it was argued that reflection is a way of rethinking and learning from experience: 'The function of reflective thought is, therefore, to transform a situation in which there is experienced obscurity, doubt, conflict, disturbance of some sort, into a situation that is clear, coherent, settled, harmonious' (Dewey, 1933: 100–1). This notion of learning from reflection was enhanced by Schön in his books on reflective practice (Schön, 1983, 1987, 1991) and promoted in his phrases 'reflection-on-action' and 'reflection-in-action'.

The value of teachers reflecting on practice has been well documented in the professional learning literature (Hatton and Smith, 1995; LaBoskey, 1994; Loughran, 1996). Baird (1992) called reflection 'a cornerstone of learning and of personal and professional development and a vehicle for teacher change', also stating that:

> To achieve change, teachers need to discover that their existing frame for understanding what happens in their classes is only one of several possible ones, and this, according to Schön, is likely to be achieved only when the teachers themselves reflect critically upon what they do and its results.
>
> (Baird, 1992: 17)

Although reflection is a powerful vehicle for teacher learning, it is an individual activity and does have limitations when used in isolation from other processes. Fendler (2003) recently critiqued the individual notion of reflection, stating that both Dewey's scientifically rational approach to reflection and Schön's intuitive approach are limited by a person's existing ways of thinking. For example, it is common to encourage teachers to write reflective journals or autobiographical narratives; however, these are often 'confessional' in nature and can reinforce existing practices:

> When the device of autobiographical narrative is considered together with the technique of self-disclosure in journal writing, the combination functions to construct the idea of teachers as a people who repeatedly confess and affirm their identity in terms of categories that reflect existing popular assumptions. This construction is a technology of the self that tends to perpetuate the status quo because the autobiographical markers are based on stereotypes and the conventions of what constitutes an autobiography are historically constructed.
>
> (Fendler, 2003: 23)

Fendler concluded that reflection may sometimes even be an undesirable practice, because it involves 'circular ways of thinking' to reinforce existing views on pedagogy, race, gender or class. Hence, reflection can be contradictory because it is 'disciplined by the very social practices and relations that the reflective process is suppose to critique' (Fendler, 2003: 21). In short, personal reflection is a powerful teacher learning process to support action learning, but conducted on its own it can be limiting. Hence, its value is enhanced with a combination of other teacher learning processes such as sharing as a community, feedback and action.

Teacher learning process 2: Community

The second process, community, relates to group members of the action learning set sharing personal anecdotes to gain a deeper understanding of the meaning of their personal experiences. This social influence on learning was also first highlighted by Dewey, who defined the notion of community as 'sharing in each other's activities and in each other's experiences because they have common ends and purposes' (Dewey, 1916). This recognition of the importance of social interactions for children's learning is also applicable to teachers' professional learning. When schools are viewed as learning communities for teachers, the key feature is the social interaction with colleagues to share ideas embodied in phrases such as 'shared decision making and information sharing and communication' (Darling-Hammond, 1994), 'shared vision and team learning' (Senge, 1990) and 'collective goals of understanding and judgement' (Bereiter and Scardamalia, 1993).

In the context of action learning, the value of sharing ideas as a community relates to the extent of collegiality that exists or is built up within a group. This process of sharing with the 'set' has several effects. First, it forces an individual to make public their personal reflections and insights. Second, the process of sharing these experiences confirms or disconfirms personal interpretations, which creates a stimulus for further reflection. This can be assisted by having colleagues in the group who understand the context but may have different perspectives. Third, more motivation is involved to try an initiative in teaching if the resultant action is to be made public at a later meeting. Revans also recognised that action learning was fundamentally a social process and that the essence of an action learning set was the sharing of ideas and experiences as a community:

> Action learning, in simple English, becomes a social process; a lot of people start to learn with and from each other, and a learning community comes into being and there is overwhelming evidence that this community will long survive the official project itself . . . In summary, therefore, an action learning programme needs at least a major problem about which something ought to be done . . . In addition to these, it also needs membership of a set of three or four organizations interested in sharing experiences and in exchanging inspirations.
>
> (Revans, 1982b: 69–70)

To promote community within a set as part of the action learning process there can be different levels of collegiality. First, the members may pair up as action learning 'buddies'. This is especially important to allow continuity in the conversations whereby teachers who work in close proximity to each other can chat to each other on a daily basis or several times a week. Second, the complete action learning set or team needs to meet regularly, for example, every two or three weeks, to build trust and keep the continuity of sharing ideas relating to their experiences about actions they are trying in the classroom. These meetings discuss the personal reflections of each participant, brainstorm ideas for an action plan and then look forward to hearing the results of the action plan at subsequent meetings. Hence, developing a culture of sharing among the small team is consistent with the phrase that 'six heads are better than one'. Moreover, it takes time for teachers to feel comfortable to share their experiences, both positive and negative, and to develop confidence and procedures in the group so that feedback will be constructive, not destructive.

Teacher learning process 3: Action

The third process, action, means that participants try out ideas that have been generated by personal reflection and refined in community discussions.

Learning by doing or experimenting with ideas is also not a new concept. It was one of the main tenets in Dewey's (1938) theory of learning through experience and Kolb's (1984) experiential learning cycle. The implication is that trying out ideas as actions gives them more meaning because of the understanding gained from knowing the consequences of the actions. The idea for the action may be part of a team project that is the focus of the action learning, or may be something unique to the specific team member. The result of this action becomes the topic for subsequent reflection and discussion at the next action learning meeting. Hence, the action is the outcome of the dynamic relationship between the teacher learning processes in an action learning set.

For example, each teacher needs to reflect upon practice that raises a particular problem or challenge in their teaching. These personal reflections are shared with their buddy and also with the action learning team at the set meeting. At the meeting, the problem/issue is discussed, with the different possibilities being explored, and the individual is helped by the group to decide upon the best option for an action plan. This plan then becomes the focus of the action in the classroom. The teacher then reflects upon the action and shares the result with the buddy and team, and the cycle of reflection, sharing, action and change continues.

Teacher learning process 4: Feedback

The process that completes the cycle of action learning is feedback on the efforts for change in the classroom. This feedback can come from several sources. One source can come from members of the action learning set who might observe each other teach in their classrooms. For this to occur, a level of trust needs to have developed among the group. It sometimes helps if the team member doing the observing has been asked to provide feedback on a particular aspect of teaching nominated by the teacher being observed. A second source of feedback can come from the facilitator, who may be invited by the teachers to provide some feedback on a particular aspect of their teaching.

A third source of feedback can come from the students in the classroom. This is a very powerful form of feedback, especially if the students are provided with a 'language' to articulate particular aspects of teaching and learning that may be the focus of the action learning (Hoban, 2000a). A study in a high school in NSW involved interviewing year 9 students about aspects of teaching and learning evident in different subjects. The study showed that many students did not have a good enough understanding about issues of teaching and learning to express their views. To provide students with such a 'language', the teacher was assisted to devise an observation schedule identifying aspects of teaching and learning that should be present in most science lessons. This observation schedule can be seen at the end of this chapter in Figure 4.3. The teacher initially discussed the meaning of the terms with the students and explained how to use the observation sheet. Students completed the sheet every Friday to give the teacher feedback for the week, which the teacher could reflect upon over the weekend. After the students had used the sheet for most of a school term, they did not need it any more, and some would give the teacher specific verbal feedback as they left the room, such as, 'That was a good lesson, the demonstration really helped me . . .' or 'your instructions were not clear and I still don't understand the Periodic Table'. The study found that the more the students used the observation sheet, the more articulate they were in providing feedback to the teacher about aspects of teaching and learning. This observation sheet informed the students' feedback, which sustained the teacher's reflection for over a year (Hoban and Hastings, 2006).

The synergy created

When teachers attend one-off workshops or a professional development day, attempts to implement changes in the classroom can occur, but it is more common for these experiences to reinforce existing practice and maintain the status quo. This type of learning is what Argyris and Schön (1974) called 'single-loop learning', which results in learning that tends to be routine and reactive to existing problems. In contrast, when action learning operates effectively, the four teacher learning processes interact and enhance each other. This type of teacher learning is generative, meaning that it fosters the creation of new ideas and is more likely to lead to a change in practice.

The role of the facilitator is important, as this person can assist in helping teachers to establish and maintain their teacher learning processes, especially ensuring that the teachers continue to interact as a community. Where appropriate, facilitators can scaffold the team discussions by introducing new ideas or seek new expertise from outside the group based on the emerging group needs. For example, the ideas generated by action learning are enhanced when new ideas are introduced by the facilitator or from other team members. When this injection of new ideas occurs, it 'makes dilemmas recognisable, which creates tension to resolve them' (Argyris and Schön, 1974: 97). Huberman (1995) called these new ideas, which were introduced into community discussions, 'conceptual inputs'. New ideas can occur in a variety of ways, such as through the introduction of research into the community discussions (Bell and Gilbert, 1994; Richardson, 1994), inviting views of colleagues (Baird et al., 1987; Darling-Hammond, 1994) or accessing information from professional journals, television programmes or market research (Cusins, 1995). The content and timing of such inputs could be up to the discretion and expertise of the facilitator or could be determined according to a need identified by the action learning team.

When the teacher learning processes are sustained and complement each other, teachers are able to learn dynamically through an iterative, knowledge-building process. This is achieved using multiple processes for teacher learning, by reflecting upon personal beliefs *and* confirming or disconfirming beliefs by action, *and* seeking feedback on the ideas *and,* most importantly, sharing ideas and the outcomes of actions with the action learning community. The dynamics created by action learning are similar to Argyris and Schön's (1974) notion of 'double-loop learning', which occurs in workplace settings where learning is sustained and iterative, and involves new ideas to challenge the 'status quo' of conventional practice. This type of professional learning is based on a level of trust and preparedness within a group of teacher learners to take risks by sharing ideas:

> As individuals come to feel more psychological success and more likelihood of mutual confirmation or disconfirmation, they are more likely to manifest higher self-awareness and acceptance, which leads to offering valid information, which again leads to feelings of psychological success. As groups manifest higher degrees of openness, experimentation, and emphasis on individuality, individuals in them will feel freer to provide valid information that will tend, in turn, to enhance these group characteristics. As individuals feel higher degrees of freedom of choice, trust and authenticity, they are more likely to test their assumptions publicly, which, in turn, is likely to enable others to feel higher degrees of freedom of choice, trust and authenticity − all of which makes everyone more willing to give valid information that enables individuals to test their assumptions.
>
> (Argyris and Schön, 1974: 91–2)

As such, double-loop learning is not merely 'self-sealing' that confirms existing practice and maintains the status quo. It is 'transformative', facilitating educational change in a non-linear, dynamic process (Day, 1999). Two examples of action learning are now explored to demonstrate the interactive nature of multiple teacher learning processes.

Case study 1: Action learning in a primary school

Our first case study is an action learning project that occurred in a small rural primary school, 80 km south of Sydney, Australia, in 2004. It involved six teachers as well as a facilitator and extended for a period of six months. The project goal was to develop science teaching strategies to engage boys in their lessons, although there was variation as to how this was achieved. One teacher wanted to improve boys' writing in science; another wanted to improve her students' engagement in science activities; another wanted to learn new teaching approaches; and another two wanted to improve young children's manipulation skills when using science equipment. At the beginning of the project, the six teachers and the facilitator discussed the importance of being aware of teacher learning processes and how they interact. The team and facilitator were conscious of designing their project so that there was a framework to support personal reflection, group discussion, seeking feedback and actions to be implemented.

After a period of six months, the teachers were interviewed in pairs about the outcomes and processes of their professional learning. The leader (Val) and her buddy (Rob) were the most articulate about the processes of their professional learning as recorded by the interviewer (Int). Moreover, they were able to articulate the presence of multiple teacher learning processes as follows:

INT.: What did you learn about action learning as an approach to teachers' professional learning and as a strategy for school change?

VAL.: Teachers have a tendency to work alone and one of the huge benefits of this action learning process has been the social support that we have created in the team. We know that learning is a social activity but we very rarely set up a scenario in a school to provide ourselves with that type of learning and the action learning processes do that. So I have got my buddy and you are not working on your own behind the closed door as teachers have a tendency to do, especially when you are trying something new. When you try something new it's easy to share the successes but it is not so easy to share it when things goes wrong. This process allows for that so that any mistakes all become part of the learning cycle. You share, then you reflect and then you move it onto the next step to another change.

ROB.: I think time was a big issue. The school is naturally a very busy place and teachers have trouble fitting everything in and they take on so many things. But having gone through this process it has made it very obvious that we do need to take the time to reflect, and talk and share what we are doing and have other people observing what we are doing and giving us ideas. I think it is a really valuable thing for me.

VAL.: The professional dialogue and being able to observe each other and observe each other's students. Time to hunt up any resources that we are looking for and actually funding it so that you are given the time and you are constantly trying not to make extra time, you just run out of extra time so that whole process by building in the learning and time for learning was really important.

INT.: So what do you understand by the so-called action learning processes?

VAL.: It's really the application of the learning processes that we really know so well to teacher learning. The idea that you can look at something, observe something, think about it, do a bit of research on it, reflect on it, talk about it with another colleague, develop something to try, try

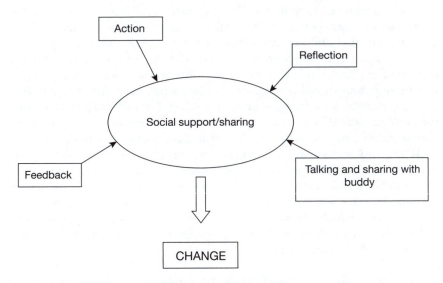

Figure 4.1 Action learning processes in a primary school

it and then reflect back on that, you know share it with another person, make a change to it, try it again, that whole learning cycle is the action learning cycle.

Figure 4.1 is a representation of how the teachers described the processes of their professional learning that they explained in their interview transcript.

Importantly, both these teachers identified not only that it was a combination of teacher learning processes that sustained their professional learning, but that it was also having time (as funded by the project) for the processes to interact. In effect, having time to reflect, share ideas and implement new ideas in action is a condition to enable the teacher learning processes to operate synergistically.

Case study 2: Action learning in a high school science faculty

This second case study involved a professional learning framework based on action learning that lasted for two years, from 1995 to 1996, in a rural high school 300 km west of Sydney (Hoban *et al.*, 1997). There were only four people involved in the study – three science teachers who made up the small faculty and the facilitator. The three teachers had spent a few weeks writing in a journal to reflect on the question of why they teach the way they do, and each was keen to explore some new ideas about science teaching. One of the unusual aspects of this project was that the teachers were keen to get feedback on their teaching from their own grade 9 students. So, the facilitator interviewed ten grade 9 students from each of the teachers' science classes and then collated the key comments about teaching and learning by re-recording them onto 'student tapes'. The students were interviewed about aspects of teaching and learning across different subjects. This provided insight into educational ideas used in other subjects, of which the science teachers may not have been aware. The teachers listened to these tapes over the two-year period as a source of feedback on their teaching. The facilitator also introduced new ideas in the context of discussions held by the teachers.

At the end of the two-year project, the teachers held two meetings to devise a model that represented the process of their action learning, as shown in Figure 4.2 (Hoban, 1996). The teachers were clear that what started the process was reflecting on their own practice in light of listening to the student tapes, which allowed them to compare their ideas about teaching and learning with those of their own students. During the first meeting, the head of the department stated:

> The thing that starts you off is the combination of listening to the student tapes and having the opportunity to reflect on your own performance and to put down what you think about teaching onto tape in our interviews. Now, all of that was really important because it's like a starting point, it uses something to base what you're doing on.
>
> (Geoff, head teacher, Science Department)

As the teachers continued to reflect, listen to the student tapes and share experiences with colleagues, they generated ideas for actions to try to implement in their practice. Rather than as a one-off event, the personal reflection and discussion with colleagues continued as they developed into a community who shared experiences and ideas for the common purpose of improving their practice. In their second meeting, Geoff described the model:

> The important thing was that it continued over time and all the time we were coming back to these, the reflection, discussion, the tapes, and we kept going back to these inputs that came in. And then other things came in from the side, your input, your views, things like that, all taken on board. The collegiality, talking to the others, working towards a common purpose that encourages you because you tend to lose the plot of it in the day-to-day hurly-burly.
>
> (Geoff, head teacher, Science Department)

Having reflected on their teaching, listened further to the student tapes and shared experiences with their colleagues, the teachers then started to think about change. They tried out ideas in their classrooms and monitored student feedback, which they discussed in subsequent meetings. Geoff stated:

What happens then is you start to think about change and then what happens is you look at change and then you get the feedback . . . from the students, how you feel it's going, from the collegiality again, from your colleagues talking it over.

(Geoff, head teacher, Science Department)

What the teachers emphasised was that the progression of their learning was based on a combination of processes that acted together according to the cycle of action learning:

The basis of it is that skeleton, that starting point – the student tapes and your own opportunities for reflection, and then the change, feedback, more reflection, change, feedback, that cycle all the time bringing in ideas from outside, from other inputs, from your colleagues, from you and so on. And I think if any of these factors had been missing, then it wouldn't have worked.

(Geoff, head teacher, Science Department)

The teachers described the professional learning process as a 'cycle of change' because their learning was linked to an action learning framework that was different from conventional professional development programmes that present ideas in isolation to their practice. Geoff summarised this framework for the group:

So the whole thing becomes a cycle of change where you start with the student tapes and you start to reflect on the various aspects that you practise and you bring in all these external influences and you bring them together in your head and try work out what you're going to do yourself in a classroom. And the important thing about it is that, and this is where it is different to other forms of professional development and this is why it's caused change, is that it is continually reinforced because it is ongoing and because it has this framework that we keep coming back to, we feel as though we're part of a project and part of a process that's ongoing and not short-term. It's not a stick a finger in the dyke here, stick another finger in the dyke there, learn about literacy here, learn about assessment there – it's a whole integrated package.

(Geoff, head teacher, Science Department)

In summary, the combination of the teacher learning processes – personal reflection, group discussion, student interviews, action and student feedback – acted synergistically in an action learning framework, resulting in the teachers being continually engaged in learning about their own practice. And the key to promote change was that the processes were interrelated. Figure 4.2 shows the diagrammatic model that the teachers devised to represent their action learning over the two years.

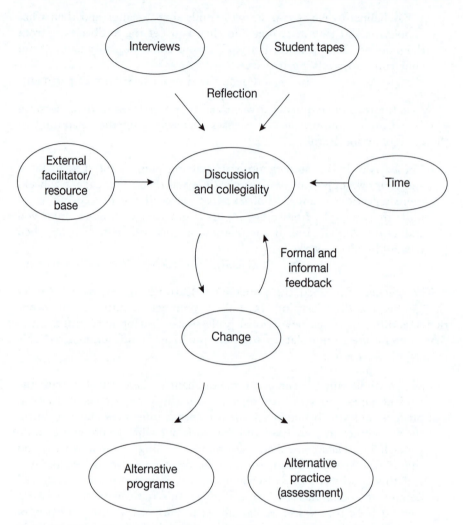

Figure 4.2 Action learning processes in a secondary science department

An interesting development occurred near the end of the two-year period. By this time the feedback on the student tapes had less meaning, because the teachers had changed their practice significantly. The teachers wanted new feedback, so they asked the students to fill in 'learning logs' about what and how they were learning in science. They encouraged the students to do this once a week, at the end of the science lesson on Fridays. This continued for six months, but the teachers found that the children were not very articulate in their feedback because they did not have a 'language' to describe the teaching and learning mechanisms. To address this issue, as mentioned earlier, one of the teachers worked with the facilitator to devise an 'observation sheet' to seek student feedback (see Figure 4.3 overleaf). This observation sheet gave year 9 students a 'language' to discuss issues of teaching and learning and worked effectively over a period of twelve months. In 1997, all three teachers won State awards for excellence in teaching. Two of them are now high school principals, and one is the head teacher of a science department. The three teachers still keep in contact.

Common themes

Although these two case studies come from two different settings, a primary school and a high school, there are some strong similarities. First, central to the teacher learning process of action learning is the sense of sharing experiences promoted by the teacher learning process of 'community'. This is represented in the 'social support/sharing' at the centre of Figure 4.1 for the primary school teachers and in the 'discussion and collegiality' at the centre of Figure 4.2 for the high school teachers. In both cases, the other teacher learning processes – reflection, action and feedback – all enhanced the group discussions by promoting a sense of honesty and trust that is key to developing a community. Therefore, the personal reflections, actions and feedback provided the content for reporting back to the group to share and seek new ideas into the next stage of action learning.

Another point raised by both the primary and secondary teachers was the importance of allocating time for the process to occur. In both projects, there was some funding available to free some time for the teachers to reflect on their practice, try some action and seek feedback. Although time is not considered to be a process of teacher learning in itself, it is a key condition required to activate and connect the teacher learning processes. The importance of providing teachers with time to participate in these processes cannot be overstated. Hence, establishing an action learning team is not a simple procedure and it is very different to a one-off professional development workshop or in-service day.

Conclusion

This chapter has explained the four main teacher learning processes under-pinning action learning – reflection, community, action and feedback – and used two case studies to show how they interrelate. The key message is that, for action learning to operate, it needs all of the processes operating, because it is their interaction that sustains and scaffolds teachers' professional learning. Moreover, the interaction is dynamic and generative, meaning that the teacher learning processes enhance and reinforce each other, leading to new ideas to

My Learning Sheet – Date:

....

In the last week I have learned the following things in Science (think of ways of doing things, facts and figures, words and their spelling, something you are good at in Science):

(a) ....

....

(b) ....

....

(c) ....

....

(d) ....

....

(e) ....

....

Last week in Science I didn't do so well at learning:

(a) ....

....

(b) ....

....

(c) ....

....

(d) ....

....

What sorts of things that the teacher has done have helped you to learn in Science this week:
1. Explanations from the teacher
2. Practicing something
3. Doing experiments
4. Class discussion
5. Individual help from the teacher
6. Making written notes
7. A demonstration
8. Anything else?

....

....

....

What sorts of things have you done in Science to help you learn?
1. Listened in class
2. Had a guess at something and tested if it worked
3. Remembered things I had learned before
4. Drew a picture or diagram
5. Asked friends
6. Asked the teacher
7. Asked at home
8. Watched someone else doing something
9. Wrote notes in my own words
10. Did a summary

....

....

....

What sorts of things have your classmates done to help you learn?
1. Worked well in a group with me
2. Let me compare my work with their work
3. Paid attention when I wanted to listen to someone else
4. Told me how to do something when I needed help
5. Let me watch them do something

....

....

....

Figure 4.3 Science lesson observation

try out in classrooms. Like a synergy, the sum of the processes becomes greater than each one acting in isolation. If any one of the teacher learning processes is not operating, it may stall or stagger the process, because each one enhances the others.

Action learning involves a team of committed teachers and a facilitator who can help drive the process. If the team members and the facilitator understand the teachers' learning processes and the necessary conditions, they are more likely to be successful with the type of 'double-loop learning' promoted by action learning. The challenges are significant to initiate and sustain action learning, but the benefits for teacher change are also significant. The next chapter will reinforce the importance of community in action learning, and Chapter 9 will more clearly articulate a model for sustaining teachers' professional learning.

Chapter 5

Community

Community has become an almost all-pervading concept in teacher professional learning:

> The word community is at risk of losing its meaning. From the prevalence of terms such as 'communities of learners', 'discourse communities', and 'learning communities' to 'school community', 'teacher community', or 'communities of practice', it is clear that community has become an obligatory appendage to every educational innovation. Yet aside from linguistic kinship, it is not clear what features, if any, are shared across terms. What makes teacher community different from a gathering of teachers?
>
> (Grossman and Wineburg, 2000: 6)

Although a 'professional' community remains an ambiguous notion, manifesting itself in various guises, it has important implications for action learning. This chapter discusses the synergy between action learning and professional community formation. In some schools, action learning has been successful in initiating or promoting teacher learning. In some instances, community seems to be an essential antecedent for this. In others, action learning acts as a catalyst in community formation. In still others, various barriers operate to inhibit effective collaboration. Some of these barriers may be inherent in action learning's demands for the open exchange of experiences, interdependence and related gathering of evidence (Aubusson *et al.*, 2007). The interaction between action learning and community formation offers insights into ways that the building of community, which is important in this type of professional learning, can be enhanced and it also raises questions about idealised representations of community.

Community, learning and project teams

The idea of a professional learning community (Darling-Hammond, 1998; DuFour, 2004; Ewing, 2002; Hargreaves, 2007a) has become a popular and prevailing catch cry as a mechanism for school improvement. Unfortunately, the term has been used 'to describe every imaginable combination of individuals with an interest in education . . . (and) so ubiquitously that it is in danger of losing all meaning' (DuFour, 2004: 6). As already mentioned, a set is the small group of people that engages in action learning (Revans, 1983b). In schools, however, principals, team leaders and executive rarely talk in terms of a set, but often refer to a learning team or professional learning community (Aubusson et al., 2006). This use of language suggests that notions of professional learning that have been widely reported in education and taken up by educational organisations have been grafted on to the relatively recent addition to school improvement: action learning. Action learning is often expected not only to play a role in teacher development, changing practices, improving student learning and producing higher test scores, but also to create a new (or enhance an existing) professional learning community. Hence, we will consider what constitutes a professional learning community before elaborating on its relationship with action learning.

A professional community of learners has much in common with a 'community of practice' (Wenger, 1998), a 'knowledge building community' (Bereiter and Scardamalia, 1993) and a 'learning organisation' (Senge, 1990). They share features including: conversation seeking understanding of matters of significance to the community; collective expertise surpassing that of individuals; scrutiny of beliefs, practices and outcomes; an improvement orientation; and mutual respect (Aubusson et al., 2006; Bereiter and Scardamalia, 1993; Erickson et al., 2005; Wenger, 1998). This is not to say that there are not differences. For example, some place an emphasis on the organisation as the framework for the learning group (e.g. Retallick, 1997). Others prefer the connotations of community emphasising socially mediated aspects of membership and activity: 'Communities are organised around relationships and ideas . . . [in] the school as learning community, connections are governed more by social covenants than by social contracts . . . [they] function as social organisations that are distinct from formal organisations' (Sergiovanni, 1999: 15). Similarly, it has been argued that the concept of 'community' is a good description of teachers' professional learning groups, owing to the collegiality that often arises in school cultures (Groundwater-Smith, 1999a: 212).

Hodkinson and Hodkinson (2003) contrast a school teacher as occupant of education as a field of practice (sometimes described as a community) with the teacher as member of a tight community, 'mutually engaged in a shared enterprise with an agreed repertoire of actions and focused on collabo-rative learning, such as community of practice'. The importance of community has often been stressed (Wenger et al., 2002; Wenger and Snyder, 2000), because a community of practice is united not as an organisational unit but by the shared learning and interests of its membership. It is informally bound together and it exists because participation is valued by its members. The community operates a social learning system, where the characteristics of a teacher professional community include: collaboration, deprivatisation of practice, reflective dialogue, pedagogical leadership and shared responsibilities, as well as deliberation to clarify and critique values, assumptions, beliefs, understanding of educational positions and working principles (Andrews and Lewis, 2002: 251). Andrews and Lewis emphasise the collective agreement and shared understanding on what needs to be done and how it is to be done.

A professional learning community is not a new way to establish a functional unit in an organisation or to manage a project. It is a social system of knowledge production and exchange among a group that shares a field of practice in which it has expertise and about which it interacts, seeking to improve the ways things are done. Such a learning community may engage in a project or specific task, but its existence is not limited to or defined by the project. Rather, the nature of the community of practice is defined by its knowledge and expertise. A community of practice can be contrasted with a project team, because the community 'does not appear the minute a project is started and does not disappear with the end of a task. It takes a while to come into being and may live long after a project is completed or an official team has disbanded' (Wenger, 1998: 3). Wenger (1998) stresses the distinction between a community of practice and a project team, arguing that a community has an existence, identity and professional relationships beyond those of a project team. There are inherent differences in longevity, flexibility of membership, activity and knowledge management. It is useful to contrast this notion of community with that of a team of teachers established for a project, with its work defined by a proposal with set goals and a schedule of planned actions.

In discussions on professional learning, the explicit distinction made between team and community suggests there is a need to consider the nature of teacher learning teams. Johnson (1999: 34–8) sought to 'rethink' and clarify the meaning of teacher leaning teams. Effective learning teams were identified as those that:

- require a reason to exist, such as a specific project, for members to learn and engage in professional collaboration;
- focus on producing more effective learning for all students;
- make use of external and work-embedded support;
- collaborate and systematically reflect on practice;
- facilitate professional challenge, balancing high interest, high support and high cognitive demand;
- have a formal leader(s), but all members consider themselves to be change agents and leaders; and
- adapt rather than adopt change proposals, crafting them to team-determined needs.

There seems to have been little consistency in the use of the terms team and community in the literature. For example, Johnson's list of features for a team could also apply to a community of practice or a learning organisation. Teams, however, are more typically associated with specific projects and are often relatively small. The emphases in both team and community are on collaboration, open and frank exchange of ideas and practices, enquiry using evidence to inform and guide change, shared responsibility, reflection and action.

There has been criticism of the possible acceptance of a professional learning community as space for mere talk without action. Schmoker (2005: 136), for example, argues that:

> mere collegiality will not cut it. Discussions about curriculum issues and popular strategies may feel good but go nowhere. The right image to embrace is a group of teachers who meet regularly to share, and refine the impact of lessons and strategies continuously to help increasing numbers of students learn at higher levels.

On the other hand, this construction of professional community may overemphasise assessment outcomes without addressing big issues in learning and schooling. It could deny teacher communities influence beyond implementation in education, as well as deny them the ability to critique curriculum, testing and assessment. Embedded in notions of professional community is a demand for a practice orientation that is informed by intellectual rigour. Groundwater-Smith (1999a) perhaps captures an essential feature in her analysis of a productive school learning community. She concludes that its work is 'scholarly', positioning teaching as 'not merely a learning profession but a learned profession' (Groundwater-Smith, 1999a: 227).

This discussion does not provide a definitive distinction between a teacher learning team and professional learning community (of teachers). Nevertheless, in school-based action learning it is possible to consider some common distinctions between a team and a community for the purposes of our discussion on action learning. Our studies of school action learning suggest that the term team ably describes the small groups of teachers (and sometimes others such as parents, consultants, critical friends or academics) working closely together on a project. While these teams are not commonplace and often vary in their degree of success, they are identifiable in many schools. The teams often engage in very specific projects or tasks.

An action learning set has features in common with both a project team and a community as described here. Like a team, a set often takes on projects, but the scope of its learning is not limited to, or defined by, the project. A set has a life and *raison d'être* beyond the project. Therefore, an action learning set is more than a project team. While a set may undertake a project, it has a longer-term engagement in improvement-aimed professional learning.

Thus, a set operates much like a community. It has a sense of community, although it is often smaller than most conceptions of community. Furthermore, a community may include a number of sets.

To highlight the variable approaches that are possible, a number of common ways in which teachers have worked together in case studies that we have conducted are outlined below:

- Groups of teachers gather to manage and administer curriculum, teaching and learning.
- Colleagues gather to engage in professional conversations about education issues, ideas, teaching and learning practices relevant to their school context.
- Colleagues work as a team on projects using ad hoc processes.
- Colleagues work on projects using evidence-guided processes.
- Action learning sets operate with a clear, overarching sense of purpose. They also collaborate, share knowledge, take on project(s) and engage in evidence-based practice.
- A teacher community has a project team or action learning set that periodically informs and shares experiences and ideas and stimulates engagement by others.
- A professional learning community, with a *raison d'être*, has teachers who produce and scrutinise practice-oriented knowledge and generate and test ways of doing things. This may include action learning sets with a related platform of endeavour.

It is attractive to conceive of a whole school staff as a professional learning community, but there are structural and social barriers that inhibit whole-school engagement in this way (Grossman and Wineburg, 2000). In a high school, for example, groups of teachers are often separated into faculty groups that rarely come together. The formation of a cohesive, professional community is difficult in schools because they are diverse and complex organisations (Grossman *et al.*, 2001; Huberman, 1990; Siskin, 1994), and teachers have historically operated in their classrooms as isolated entities (Lortie, 1975). Consequently, there is often little of the sharing or scrutiny of professional knowledge (Hargreaves, 2000) that might be expected among teachers charged with a collective responsibility for the education of each next generation. Yet, despite the challenges and difficulties, some schools do manage to operate as learning communities. (The 'Sustaining professional learning' chapter provides two examples.)

Action learning and the evolution of community

Two action learning initiatives currently under study serve to illustrate some of these difficulties in community formation. First, the principal of Bindi

Elementary School is experienced and instigated action learning at a previous school. In her current school, she explained that she has 'insisted all teachers participate in the action learning project', which is the approach that was taken at her previous school. While all members of staff are involved to varying degrees, it is noteworthy that the teachers are organised into small teams of five to eight teachers. Each team meets regularly and takes responsibility for two or three year groups in the school. The action learning is constructed around three teams: Team A is responsible for teaching and learning for kindergarten to year 2, Team B for years 3 and 4 and Team C for years 5 and 6. The teams are also a function of the school's organisational structure. Indeed, these age groups are a product of a centralised syllabus that lays down the curriculum according to these groupings.

In this example, the school's teachers are not so much a learning community as three loosely connected teams that may evolve into action learning sets, of which the principal is acutely aware. She states: 'We haven't got there yet . . . You have to have a community first and then a professional community that wants to work and learn together to become better at what it does.' It is also worth noting that the teams operate differently. Teams A and C have had a history of close collaboration in curriculum planning and implementation, while Team B consists of teachers who have collaborated little. In the current action learning process, according to the teachers and principal, Teams A and C have attended workshops, collaboratively agreed on actions and engaged in collective reflection on these actions. By contrast, Team B also attended the workshops, but has allocated tasks to different staff, reflecting an approach to action learning that views it as a project with a set of identifiable, discrete tasks. This view considers that each member contributes best by completing part of the project, with little interaction with other members of the team.

This example illustrates some key points related to action learning and professional community formation that have been observed in many cases. In particular, productive action learning sets often grow out of existing collaborating groups with a predisposition to share and exchange ideas and practices. It is evident that there are barriers to the formation of a whole-school action learning set or a whole-school professional learning community. Specifically, size counts, and it is challenging to establish a mechanism that permits effective professional learning for a large community. This shows that it is more difficult to establish a large professional learning community than a small one. There are systemic barriers to whole-school teams. In the case considered here, the curricula for Teams A, B and C are different. While they have a common target, improving literacy outcomes for their students, they are dealing with students of very different ages and capacities. As a consequence, the actions they take may be different and may be considered to be of little relevance across the age-based curriculum barriers. Thus, although the teachers worked with the same external adviser and dealt with the same principles of practice, such as use of hands-on materials, each group worked separately in determining what specific actions were required for their own groups of classes.

Similarly, in a second community-forming initiative in a high school, the teachers were invited to establish teacher learning teams, with one team for each year level. In this case, none of the teams had worked closely together previously, as most activities were organised within curriculum areas such as the English staff, or the history staff and so on. Since each staff group was located in its own staff room, there was little likelihood of incidental meetings and extended professional conversations between staff in different disciplines during non-teaching periods. The initiative of year-based teacher learning teams was intended to stimulate across-the-curriculum discussion and integration. Its main purpose was to enable each learning team to target specific needs and opportunities within each year cohort by teachers who taught the same students. Their existence was not defined by what was taught but by who was taught.

In this case, only one team, the year 7 team, functioned productively and continued to meet regularly throughout the year.[1] This team included three first-year-out teachers. This team chose the common goal of smoothing *their* students' transition into their new high school. They also often discussed matters of particular concern to the three beginning teachers, mainly regarding classroom and behaviour management. Thus, this team had a clear reason for being, a shared identity based on a worthy matter of common interest for which team members felt responsible. The team also provided a service to individual members by supporting the beginning teachers in classroom management. By contrast, the other year group 'teams' seemed to lack clarity about a shared project and, if the teachers needed support, they sought it in their curriculum groups. Barriers prevented the establishment of both action learning sets and a broad, inclusive professional learning community. In particular, some of the proposed teams had no reason to collaborate, and the internal organisation around subject groupings already provided support. These factors inhibited the establishment of alternative learning teams.

Despite these difficulties, action learning sets do form in schools and provide good outcomes for teachers and students. A typical outcome of action learning that we have studied has been greater collaboration and communication among teachers. This has been evident in a majority of schools that have sought to engage in action learning (Aubusson et al., 2006; Ewing et al., 2004). Teachers have often commented favourably on this (Aubusson et al., 2006); for example:

> What worked was the real team work and collaboration within the executive and between staff members that has generated professional discussion and the ability to try new ways of doing things.
>
> (Team leader on action learning in her school)

1 Year 7 is the first year in high school.

Others spoke positively of the conversations that were essential to their action learning and valued their professional dialogue, stating that it

> was invaluable to the project, bouncing ideas off each other and learning from each other . . . working together to achieve a result.

Our studies indicate that action learning brings teachers together and promotes mutual support to build a sense of community. However, staff participating in our studies reported a varying range of interactions, from schools where teachers barely engaged with each other, to those where participants worked very closely together. In Butterfly High School (Aubusson *et al.*, 2007), where peer observation was proposed as a key feature of the action learning, a team member lamented that 'the difficulty a number of teachers have in being confident enough to be self-critically reflective of their classroom practice . . . also equates to a reluctance to allow peers to observe their teaching practice'. Action learning's demands for mutual trust and respect were too great an obstacle for this group of teachers, as they preferred to retain their current safety in isolation. Consequently, the attempt to instigate action learning with peer observation fell at the first hurdle, with almost no participation, exchange of ideas nor interest in the underlying pedagogy of the action learning initiative being exhibited. On the other hand, a team at another school experienced a very high degree of interaction within the action learning team when they used peer observation. The team leader reported that there was 'a definite positive change in team members' willingness and enjoyment of shared planning, shared teaching, shared reflection and shared informed future planning, that was resultant on their sustained team teaching activities throughout the project'.

Our research has indicated that action learning teams were more likely to engage in professional conversations when all or most of their members had a shared specific activity, such as a process for reflection, a teaching strategy or a means of gathering evidence about student learning. For example, at Woodland Elementary School, the action learning team was established by two members of the executive, with little input from other staff. Initial meetings were awkward, not valued and some members exhibited a reluctance to participate. The team consisted of the two leaders, an academic advisor and four teachers. Some initial members withdrew and were replaced by others. All members of the team then tried an identical, innovative assessment task, where the teachers used hands-on experiences with small numbers of students, concurrent with an interview, to determine students' prior knowledge in mathematics. This task led to an animated and extensive discussion at a follow-up meeting. Based on this discussion, the teachers regularly collaborated to develop common lessons to implement in teaching topics. These lessons involved the implementation of an agreed pedagogical model. The teachers taught the lessons in their own classes, and this provided a 'contextual anchor' (Loughran, 1995: 431) for reflection and professional discussion. Members of the team worked with other teachers who taught classes with students of similar ages (called stages). As a consequence, a hands-on assessment activity and an interview were tried by every teacher in the school. One team member explained how the initiative had progressed:

> Each week we have a stage meeting . . . with a chance to talk about what we're up to. We talk about the lesson before we teach it and give and get advice on how to do it. We discuss the previous week's [common] lesson and . . . our teachers' journals. There's a real reward in conversations about how lessons went.

Much of the conversation involved the teachers describing and discussing anecdotes about their classroom experiences. This explains why, comparatively, the early meetings failed to generate rich discussion, as there were no specific, shared episodes of classroom experiences to discuss. The early meetings consisted of general discussion of the relatively dry set of pedagogical principles that did not address the interests of the teachers. The pedagogy that they were working with was an abstract entity that was, at best, of moderate interest to the teachers until it was rendered tangible in actual practice. It is difficult, however, to imagine how the valued professional interaction in the community that occurred later could have arisen spontaneously and fully formed at the beginning. From this experience, it seems likely that an initial commitment is required by members to carry the work through early stages of development. While it might be frustrating and seem to be of little value at the beginning, the community members gradually get to know each other and are then able to determine precisely what they want to achieve and how. In this school, like many others, the evolution of a project team towards a professional community through action learning sets is evident, but by no means complete.

Grossman *et al.* (2001) have outlined a model of the formation of a teacher professional community that is consistent with the evolution of community observed in schools where groups of teachers are engaged in action learning (see Figure 5.1). Aubusson *et al.* (2007) mapped a number of studied features of action learning against this model. It was argued that it was possible to identify many of the features that could be regarded as beginning, evolving or mature. Different teams reached levels of different dimensions according to the model. In some cases, teams did not progress beyond an early stage where the teachers discussed the project but shared little of their views of teaching or their experiences. Many teams progressed further, with extensive discourse stimulated by genuine enquiry. The development of group owner-ship and shared responsibility for their actions were also a feature of many teams, and this was typically associated with those teams that had a strong group identity. However, few action learning teams exhibited all the

Beginning   **Evolving**   **Mature**

1. Formation of group identity and norms of interaction

Beginning	Evolving	Mature
Identification with subgroup	Pseudocommunity (false sense of unity; suppression of conflict)	Identification with whole group
Individuals are interchangeable and expendable	Recognition of unique contributions of individual members	Recognition that group is enriched by multiple perspectives (sense of loss when member leaves)
Undercurrent of incivility	Open discussion of interactional norms	Development of new interactional norms
Sense of individualism overrides responsibility to group's functioning	Recognition of need for regulation of group behaviour	Communal responsibility for and regulation of group behaviour

2. Understanding difference/navigating fault lines

Beginning	Evolving	Mature
Denial of difference	Appropriation of divergence	Understanding and productive use of difference
Conflict goes backstage, hidden from view		Conflict is an expected feature of group life and dealt with openly and honestly

3. Negotiating the essential tension

Beginning	Evolving	Mature
Lack of agreement over purposes of professional community; different positions are viewed as inherently antagonistic	Begrudging willingness to let different people pursue different activities	Recognition that teacher learning and student learning are fundamentally intertwined

4. Taking communal responsibility for individuals' growth

Beginning	Evolving	Mature
Belief that teachers' responsibility is to students, not colleagues; intellectual growth is the responsibility of the individual	Recognition that colleagues are resources for one's learning	Commitment to colleagues' growth
Contributions to group are acts of individual volition	Recognition that participation is expected for all	Acceptance of rights and obligations of community membership

Figure 5.1 Model of the formation of the teacher professional community

characteristics of a particular level of development. Rather, they exhibited features across the developmental continuum, as well as exhibiting different characteristics at different times and according to different contexts and circumstances.

In the school discussed above, where lesson plans were shared and implemented, the group exhibited particular characteristics at certain stages of the project's development:

- Beginning: conflict goes backstage, hidden from view. This was evident in that members of the team described to the case study researchers points of dissatisfaction with other people or the project activities that had not been shared with the group.
- Evolving: recognition that participation is expected of all members. This was evident in that members committed to participate in meetings and agreed activities.
- Mature: recognition that the group is enriched by multiple perspectives. This was evident in comments about a colleague who chose to leave the team and in meetings where different points of view regarding the pedagogy were considered and discussed in depth.

Progress towards professional communities of learning

In some schools, teachers are able to make more progress towards forming professional learning communities than others. Important factors in action learning initiatives that contributed to transition from project groups to mature communities include having dedicated time to converse; an enquiry focus; a shared pedagogy; and commitment to shared ownership and leadership (Aubusson et al., 2007). These features are dealt with in more depth below.

Time was often emphasised as being the most important factor in establishing space for teachers to meet regularly in their action learning sets. This often requires teachers to be released from teaching and therefore it has consequent costs. For example, funds tied to teacher release 'enable us to purchase time for teachers to work together and improve their teaching. It makes ALL the difference. It is SO important in light of our overcrowded curriculum, ever-increasing demands on teacher time and increasing levels of accountability' (Action learning team member, Aubusson et al., 2006: 22; emphasis in original). A similar view has been repeatedly expressed in many case studies.

A sense of enquiry is also useful in building and growing a community, because it casts teaching and learning as problematic and open to investigation and improvement. In our experience, a spirit of problem-solving and investigation requires evidence about what is working and what is not working for teachers, and this can guide their desire to improve. Revans (1983a) elaborated on the relationship between collaboratively taking on a challenging problem and the evolution of a social system. He stressed the importance of social processes as people learn from and with each other. He also emphasised the importance of the set operating as a learning community that is willing to pose questions, take risks and engage in problem solving-driven enquiry.

At Lakeside High School, for example, the team addressed the problem of poor student literacy. To address the problem, the team conducted regular professional conversations, gathered data about literacy achievement and analysed evidence about progress related to their actions. The team grew in number and commitment because it could use evidence to convince sceptical colleagues about the success of their actions. This was also influenced by professional conversations that provided a way for teachers to learn to address what was considered an all-pervading and fundamental problem in the school. They continued gathering data, and this tangible evidence encouraged them that engagement in the process was worthwhile. In short,

> When action learning teams [have] an enquiry base for their project they were able to use data collection and discussion of evidence to initiate, perpetuate and deepen the professional relations among team members. Thus there is a reciprocal relationship between action learning and the building of an effective professional learning community.
>
> (Aubusson *et al.*, 2007: 142)

It is useful for teachers in action learning sets to adopt or adapt a shared enterprise. Similar shared actions can be an important part of knowledge exchange in some sets. In the example discussed above, all teachers used the same hands-on practical trial, using a strategy to identify students' initial understandings by employing an identical lesson activity. It is also useful if the shared actions are derived from an understood position, such as a theoretical position, pedagogy or teaching strategy. However, a universal commitment to the theoretical position or pedagogy as the best or ideal way of doing things is not required. Rather, what is essential is merely a commitment to 'give it a go', to test its worth for them and their students. There is less evidence (Aubusson *et al.*, 2007) of a requirement for an agreed theoretical orientation or theoretical position on learning, though leaders of teams sometimes articulate such a position.

Shared responsibility is an important feature of an action learning set (Aubusson *et al.*, 2006). The term responsibility is preferred to ownership here, because ownership may imply ownership of a project, with the exclusion of others. Indeed, in some cases, the strong sense of ownership by a team or a subset of members of the team was productive in that it tended to ensure the team was focused and determined to carry the project through. On the other hand, it could also result in resentment by others who felt excluded from the project or from the inner group taking carriage of the project. In many schools we have observed, it is interesting to note that teachers would often become part of the team, with a sense of obligation to assist their colleagues, or because working together seemed the right thing to do. One teacher at Hyland High School reflected on her action learning experience as follows:

> The self-directed small teams . . . in which there was congruence of the teachers' personal attributes (including commitment, perseverance and determination) contributed a shared responsibility and interdependence among teachers in each team. This made them want to press on 'to get the project done' for each other. In the longer term they knew they were 'doing it for the kids' but in the shorter term, especially when things got rough, they were doing it for each other.

This comment proved insightful because the pattern of shared responsibility was not only apparent in this school but in many schools. Teachers often continued their participation, even when they felt a little drained or worn by the added workload, because they wanted to do what was best for their students. It gave them a sense of happiness when they saw their 'students succeed', and they didn't want to be the one to 'let their team down'.

Leadership in action learning has been discussed in detail in the chapter on 'Enabling action learning: Getting started'. Here, it is sufficient to say that distributed leadership is important. So too, in specific projects undertaken by the action learning set, is the formal acceptance of leadership roles often helpful to 'get the game to happen'. This seems more important as teams grow. Very small groups up to about six or seven seem to operate effectively without designated leaders, although these often come to the fore without official designation. However, in larger groups, it is important for a leader or leaders to take on the role of overseeing meetings, reporting and organising events, as well as encouraging the intellectual work and scholarship of the team. In such an oversight role, it is important to strike a balance that ensures smooth running of the group, without taking it over. Furthermore, in schools, which often have a hierarchical management structure, the leader has an important role in managing the interface between the team and the formal organisational structures of the school. In this way, the leader seeks to ensure that formal requirements and administrative demands do not inhibit the action learning set's capacity for innovation, while at the same time ensuring it does not promote an anarchy that makes it intolerable in the system.

Our analysis of the features of an action learning set, professional learning community and learning team has established a high standard. Indeed, it is easy to see an analogy for the extensive demands made of groups judged to be accomplished professional learning communities in the criteria for being judged an 'accomplished woman' in *Pride and Prejudice* (Austen, 2008). In this novel, Mr Darcy, with Miss Bingly, describes a long and seemingly impossible list of attributes necessary for any woman to be described as 'accomplished', to which Elizabeth Bennett responds, 'I am no longer surprised at your knowing only six accomplished women. I rather wonder now at your knowing any' (Austen, 2008: 72). If this is the case with professional learning communities, it may be unsurprising then that the formation and maintenance of such communities are said to be rare (DuFour, 2004). It begs the question, are the expectations or criteria set too high and unrealistic?

It is difficult for a large school's entire staff to function effectively as a single action learning set. Yet some schools achieve something akin to this. In the chapter 'Sustaining professional learning through action learning', for example, cases are reported where schools have not only formed professional learning communities, but maintained these over a number of years. However, these tend to be the exception rather than the rule. Even if teachers are willing and able to adopt the basic tenets of functioning in a professional learning team, the management of practicalities, frequent meetings for all, scholarly enquiry and effective dialogue provide barriers that are difficult and unnecessary to surmount. It is entirely realistic, however, to expect that a school professional learning community could be effectively established as groups of action learning sets that operate as relatively independent cells, creating and exchanging knowledge about broad goals, such as how to improve attendance, written expression, numeracy, classroom behaviour or engagement among students in their school. One of the reasons action learning initiatives have failed is because they attempt to establish a large professional learning community without first developing smaller working teams.

The characteristics of professional learning communities have been described and discussed. There seems to be little to be gained in using this list to label or classify school-based groups as if there are clear points at which a group can be classified as a professional learning community or not. Rather, we have provided a set of attributes as a guide or aspiration, to inform the creation and development of groups of teachers collaborating to learn and enhance practice. Action learning can play an important role in contributing to the evolution of professional communities. Equally, a professional learning community can contribute to the formation and sustenance of action learning sets. Here it is useful to use the Grossman et al. (2001) and Wenger (1998) models of learning community and community of practice to inform the development of professional communities. It is also useful to envisage the way in which action learning can make a contribution to professional learning community formation (see Figure 5.2).

It is clear that traditional school organisations are often not fundamentally conducive to the formation of teacher professional learning communities. A group of teachers must overcome significant obstacles that inhibit their development into a professional learning community. Such obstacles include features such as isolation, lack of time, a hierarchical organisational structure,

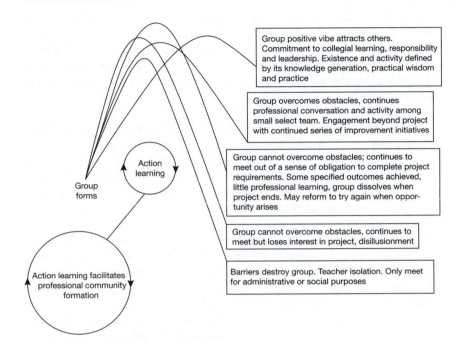

Figure 5.2 Action learning and community formation

resistance to change and an inflexible and assessment-driven curriculum. These barriers are not there to make it difficult or to strive to oppose the community. They just happen to exist in the school system or culture. There seems to be a nebulous, critical pivot point in community formation. This point is context specific and varies in different schools. Before this point, the community struggles and must exert great and sustained effort to progress towards maturity. After this point, a mature community becomes normal, self-sustaining and part of the school organisation, rather than acting in opposition to it. Figure 5.2 attempts to represent this and to indicate how action learning may make it easier for groups of teachers to survive the challenges and to reach and pass the pivot point.

Conclusion

We do not suggest that action learning makes professional community formation inevitable or easy. Our experience has been similar to that described by Grossman *et al.* (2001: 11):

> When we turn to the school level (particularly the high school), the most logical venue for day-to-day community, we run into a series of

structural, cultural, and vocational impediments. The simple fact is that in the typical American high school the structures for on-going intellectual community do not exist. One of the peculiarities of the high school, from the teacher's perspective, is that learning aimed at deepening knowledge of the subject matters of instruction must be done outside of the workplace . . .

Yet, we have noted that action learning and its activities can facilitate professional learning community formation and enable teachers to ignore, cope with or modify the many things that inhibit their professional learning and practice. Groups of teachers and whole-school staff achieve different levels of community, learning and activity. The achievements and developments need to be recognised and celebrated. A model of the evolution of a professional learning community is useful as it can be used to advise on processes that may contribute to their development. Action learning is one process that appears to operate synergistically with community formation. Understanding of both action learning and the nature of community therefore provides guidance for those who seek to create genuine opportunities for prolonged professional learning among teachers in schools.

The next chapter explores the role an external partner may play in action learning. Among other things, the examination of this role helps to illustrate the benefits of conceiving and creating a learning community with membership beyond that of the school staff alone.

Chapter 6

Facilitating action learning: the academic partner's role

> ... the role of the academic partner is critical in supporting the teachers
> in finding a focus, in providing resources such as teaching and learning
> materials and research, and facilitating workshops.
>
> (Ewing *et al.*, 2004: 80)

This chapter examines two aspects of external assistance that can be provided to schools to aid the action learning process, focusing in particular
on the role of an academic partner. It begins with a brief contextualisa-
tion of some bigger-picture issues that may impact on a school interested
in a change process, and then examine the role system personnel can play
in funding, framing and developing a system or regional action learning
project's parameters. We also examine how system personnel can support
action learning.

The main part of the chapter, however, explores the crucial role that an
external partner can play as a critical friend in facilitating action learning in
a school or other educational institution. As noted earlier, this is a departure
from Revans' original conceptualisation of how action learning processes
would function. External partners can be seen as 'sociocultural tools' (Putnam
and Borko, 2000; Wertsch and Rupert, 1993): their input can change both
the action learning process and ways of thinking of other team members. At
the same time, the external partner's ideas and understandings can also be
changed by the action learning process and other team members' perspectives.
Views from both school action learning teams and academic partners discussed
to explore this concept further. We also suggest some frameworks for working
productively with external partners, based on our experiences. It is clear from
these experiences, as well as the research literature, that school action learning
teams can benefit significantly from external assistance to achieve their goals
(e.g. Zeichner, 2003).

External assistance in system-wide action learning projects

As we have already seen, while a number of teachers and executives from any individual school may form an action learning set or team to work on individual concerns, they may also establish a team to examine a particular school issue or problem. This may, of course, be established without outside assistance. External factors can and often do play an important role, at least initially, in triggering, funding and assisting such a project. Frequently, a government department, system, educational organisation or agency establishes some kind of reform agenda to advance its particular goals or interests. Funding and other resources to encourage school participation in such an agenda are often made available. Currently in Iceland, for example, the government inner-city educational system in Reykjavik and the University of Iceland are working on a joint research project that will enable schools to participate in one of a number of priority reform agendas. These include parent involvement in children's literacy development in disadvantaged communities; special education inclusion in the classroom; and the use of information communication technology (ICT) as a learning tool.

Similarly, over the last fifteen years in Australia, there has been an increasing interest and involvement from systems in projects using action leaning for school and teacher professional development. These have been aimed at the concept of quality teaching and, hence, over time, the improvement of student learning outcomes. The Australian Government's Quality Teaching Programme, for example, has provided each state and sector with millions of dollars of funding since 2003, for projects in a range of priority areas, including literacy, numeracy, science and technology, indigenous education, civics and values. Schools in NSW, Australia, have been able to apply to fund projects focused around state and national projects such as teacher accreditation standards; consistency of teacher judgement; building the capacity of early career teachers; and learning in the middle years of schooling, including transition from primary to high school. One project, has investigated the application of the NSW Department of Education and Training (DET) quality teaching model of pedagogy, which was released as a discussion paper in 2003 (NSW DET, 2003). Many schools chosen to be involved in these projects have welcomed this renewed focus on teaching and learning. The large majority of these projects have employed action learning processes and involved an external academic partner.

In establishing such system-wide action learning programmes, an external advisory group and a 'hands-on' system-level project manager have been vital in helping to frame the focus of the projects, both more generally and in different school contexts (Ewing et al., 2004). This external team can work with individual school teams to ensure their project not only addresses each of the funding application's criteria, but is strategically focused and not too nebulous or restrictive. They can also facilitate the sharing of ideas between different schools applying for funding, either communicating electronically or through sharing conferences. The rationale behind the individual school project, its consistency with the particular funding programme's objectives and criteria, a realistic timeframe, accountability structures and the funding of a project manager with appropriate interpersonal skills, are all important system factors influencing whether individual school action learning projects move beyond initial planning phases. Resources and access to appropriate ICT tools are also essential if individual projects are to be shared more widely in the education community.

Once an individual school action learning process commences, the role of an external partner can be extremely valuable in helping the project take shape, gather momentum and achieve its goals. The next section explores the competencies, potential roles and qualities of such a partner, as well as the contributions they can make to the action learning process.

External partner: Coach, advisor or critical friend?

> . . . his involvement with us has been of great benefit and has demonstrated that outside expertise located in university research-based environments when employed with due respect for teachers and their knowledge and experience, reinvigorates knowledge and opens the way for recognition of the potential of school/university links in current practice rather than only in pre-service education.
>
> (Principal, Plains Elementary School, in Ewing *et al.*, 2005)

This quotation from the principal of a rural school that participated in the NSW public system-wide project described above (Ewing *et al.*, 2004), provides a valuable assessment of the role an external advisor can play in the action learning process. She draws attention to the way an authentic school and university partnership is made possible through such a relationship.

In developing a professional learning community, research literature frequently cites the importance of the involvement of an advisor who is both external to the day-to-day activities and enterprise of a school and also able to understand the needs and experiences of teachers (e.g. Ewing, 2002; Yeatman and Sachs, 1995). Termed variously in the school literature 'external partner', 'academic partner', 'facilitator', 'learning coach', 'learning advisor', 'critical friend' or 'mediator', this important role is by no means confined to action learning projects and processes. In fact, it is not one originally conceived by Revans (Marsick, 2002) in relation to action learning teams. Revans (1982a) asserts that it is inevitable that a 'learning coach' will dominate the process, often teaching too much. In contrast, Marsick (2002) uses the concept of 'Action Reflection Learning' and emphasises that a 'set advisor' or learning coach will, if necessary, 'startle their [action learning] set members into deep questioning and reflection' and thus help them challenge the things they take for granted (Marsick, 2002: 305).

While not mandatory, an appropriate and carefully selected external partner has the potential to enable a distancing from and scrutiny of specific actions and personal beliefs in a particular school context. Teachers can have the opportunity to give voice to their thinking and be heard sympathetically in a constructive and critical manner by such a partner: 'To have some insight into our actions and why we act the way we do we require a mirror, someone whom we trust but can challenge, reflect and confront us with our behaviour' (Smith, 1995: 3).

In addition, Valli (1992: 189) underlines the need for teachers to dialogue with others, as well as themselves, in any reflective process that moves beyond a mere retelling or description of what is happening or what has been implemented as an action learning process unfolds. This is based on the long-standing assertion that ongoing teacher professional learning is dependent on a greater emphasis on professional dialogue and reflection to help reformulate teacher experiences and understandings (Schön, 1983, 1987). It must also be emphasised that dialogue is a two-way process, which means an external partner is not just there to listen and provide their response, reaction or evaluative comment on what has been shared. They can also facilitate focused planning, the shaping of ideas, active listening and opportunities to reflect ideas back to the team, providing expertise where appropriate. For example, when necessary, they may need to play 'devil's advocate'.

External academic partners can have the opportunity to learn just as much from the process as the school participants if they take a reciprocal approach. This reciprocity is an outcome that is often not sufficiently articulated when considering the role of an external partner.

This suggests that the term 'critical friend' is probably the most appropriate one for an external partner invited to join a school action learning team. In many cases, this will be an academic or consultant with some expertise relevant to the focus of the action learning. While the term 'critical friend' has become commonplace in educational literature and has often been used in relation to pre-service teacher education (e.g. Hatton and Smith, 1994: Smith, 1999), it is important to define this term explicitly. As Koo (2002) and Hill (2002) both argue, the term 'critical friend' can seem like an oxymoron – how can a person be simultaneously a friend and critic? This aside, the concept of 'friend' implies someone who will listen and is trusted enough by colleagues for them to take risks in revealing what actually happened or how they really felt, while the concept of 'critical' implies that the relationship is sufficiently robust to cope with questions and differing viewpoints. Such a person can confront issues that have the potential to be taken for granted or go unnoticed by the school community. This enables their perspective to balance any potential parochialism or insularity within a particular school culture.

Setting the ground rules

It is important in any school context that all members of the team, including the external partner, explicitly negotiate both the ground rules and expectations of the external partner's involvement in the project. In particular, how they enter and exit from the process, the time to be committed by the partner and the limits of their role must be considered. At the same time, the expectations and roles of a critical friend may evolve or change quite dramatically as the process progresses. For example, initially the critical friend may be invited to be a sounding board to respond to the preliminary scoping of an action learning process. As this develops, they may be able to share their expertise around a particular issue or provide a research perspective to assist with gathering evidence, analysing data and assessing outcomes. At other times, they may need to raise problems not yet considered by the team. Later, they may be asked to help keep the process on track against other competing school demands, or to facilitate or scaffold the reflective phases or report writing where required. They may also be able to help in structuring a project to ensure that sustainability of the project is possible.

External advisors may be drawn from universities or from an education system. If they are academics, the university employer must understand and value the role that they can play in such an action learning process, so that the academic will have time to be involved, for example, in school meetings. Not all academics are suitable as critical friends in an action learning process. They must have a commitment to action learning as a professional learning process and they must be ready to cast traditional academic notions of 'expert' and reputation to one side. In other contexts, academics are often expected to control the direction of research projects, rather than facilitate them. Therefore, if an academic is going to be involved in an action learning school team, they must understand that they will not be controlling the action learning process. This does not imply that the academic's expert knowledge in a particular area or more generally will not be utilised or respected, but this knowledge will not be privileged above that of the teachers in the action learning team. Teachers usually have very strong contextualised knowledge about the particular school and community. Bringing together both local and external expertise is one of the reasons why action learning can be so powerful.

In setting out the credentials needed by an external partner, Hill (2002) advocates a set of competencies that includes:

- knowledge about developing a critical framework;
- well-developed skills in responding, including allowing opportunities for silences;
- scholarly reframing;
- investigative reframing;

- big-picture framing; and
- the ability to encourage team members.

Others have cited knowledge or expertise in relevant subject/content area(s) as being necessary for an external partner to possess; however, this is not always viewed as essential. Writing from a business management perspective, Lyons (2003) provides more general attributes. He terms the 'high C's' of partnership: *Communication and collaboration, Credibility of relationships, Commitment, Critique* and *Community*. Obviously, if using action learning, a critical friend will also need to have a clear understanding of the action learning process and its framework.

While competency lists similar to those above may be helpful, they can also imply that the action learning team does not already have these skills and that the external partner is compensating or providing for these 'deficits'. The external partner's facilitation role must be emphasised, and they must never be viewed as the 'expert' (Revans, 1982a) or the one who will be able to provide the solutions to a particular issue or concern. The relationship must be seen to be a mutually beneficial partnership, one in which the external partner grows and develops alongside other team members. All knowledge needs to be valued, and, as indicated earlier, at all times in a school action learning process, the principle of teacher-led professional learning must be respected and maintained.

Establishing a relationship

Any relationship needs time to develop and deepen. The external partner may have already had a relationship with the school or with individual teachers in the school in the past. If so, the action learning team may be able to start where they left off in an earlier process. If not, the external partner will need time to find their place in the school and in the team, and to develop acceptance and trust from the team members and the school community more generally.

In one primary school, an action learning team member acknowledged at the end of the first year of the process that she had deliberately invited the external partner into her kindergarten classroom to team teach, to 'set her up'. She thought the partner would find it difficult to put her ideas into practice in a kindergarten classroom. Ultimately, as the project and the relationship developed, the teacher readily admitted, to the team and more publicly, that she had learned a great deal from the process. She commented that she actually had underestimated what kindergarten children could do for over twenty years. This demonstrates the evolving relationship, but also has much to say about the level of honesty and trust that had developed over time between the teacher and the academic partner.

Time will also need to be spent in outlining the particular issue, problem or dilemma to the external partner. Opportunities to clarify the academic partner's understanding of the project, its purpose and the roles of other members of the project team will also need to be provided. This in turn may lead to questions that other team members have not yet identified or clarified for themselves.

Project team perspectives on potential contributions of an external partner

As suggested above, various roles may be undertaken by the academic partner at different times during the action learning process. Initially, for example, the team may benefit from a different perspective in sequencing, shaping the plan or implementing the process. In helping develop a mutually supportive and collegial team, an external partner must demonstrate that he or she respects the knowledge of the school team members. Excellent interpersonal skills are therefore important.

The following quotes are taken from excerpts from various action learning case studies (Ewing *et al.*, 2004). They provide insights from the perspectives of action learning team participants, illustrating the valuable contribution they perceived their external partners had brought to different aspects of the process. Comments have been organised according to some of the factors discussed above.

Shaping the plan: Our academic partner helped us shape our plan – he suggested the team target one or two achievable components . . . think big but start small and personal.

He helped us break down the 'big ideas' and challenged us to step outside our comfort zones.

Collegiality: He was incisive, understanding, helpful with resources, prepared to observe in classrooms. He kept us together and focused on what we wanted to get out of the project . . . We never felt threatened.

Affirms knowledge that teachers already possess: . . . his respect for our knowledge and what we had to offer was vital to the success of the project . . .

Communication skills: . . . an excellent communicator who was able to bridge the artificialities . . . and provide the link between the jargon and the reality.

The fact that she came and sat and talked with us at lunch and knew the nitty gritty of the classroom.

While these comments are all very positive, the external partner's role can sometimes be very challenging. They may be required to effect difficult interventions to ensure that a particular action learning process gets back on track. In one example that spanned three schools, a project was in danger of disintegrating because the three principals had three different conceptual-isations of the major issues being explored. In addition, rather than sharing the project design with the team they envisaged would implement it, they had applied for funding and nominated team members without any discussion. Once enlisted (or co-opted) rather than invited, the team members in each school became increasingly angry and confused about what the project was about and what was expected of them. The academic partner needed to spend time in each of the schools, meeting with the sub-teams individually, listening to these concerns, enabling the team members to develop their own action learning process and then mediating with the principals to find a way forward. While in this case there was a successful outcome, one of the difficulties faced by external partners is that they actually have little power to make things happen in such a situation – they can only suggest possibilities. And when such an initiative spans three different school cultures and sets of political agendas, the negotiation role can become highly complex.

External partner perspectives on frameworks for working productively

To date there has been little systematic research into the role that external partners have played in the action learning process from the perspectives of the external partners' experiences. Our own experiences as academic partners have generally been very positive. We see the opportunity to work with school action learning teams as symbiotic and have all gained much know-ledge and understanding from our experiences (e.g. Ewing, 2002, 2006, 2008; Ewing et al., 2004; Aubusson et al., 2006). Reynolds et al. (2005), who worked as academic partners on a number of separate action learning projects, monitored their own learning journeys and mentored each other during the process. Partly because each joined their respective action learning teams after the schools had secured approval and funding, they concluded that establishing their own credibility, negotiating their roles and acquiring skills for the job were strong foci early in the process. In addition, they commented that 'emotionally it was a bit of a roller coaster ride for the academic partners – a ride that became less tumultuous as the project proceeded or at least as the players, tasks and expectations became clearer' (Reynolds et al., 2005: 7). As the projects developed, however, each noted that they experienced a sense of achievement and growth in their own self-esteem. One partner commented that she would have liked 'feedback about my input and efforts' (Reynolds et al., 2005: 9). As the projects came to an end, the academic partners felt that 'the key to improving the academic partner/school partner collaboration could perhaps be seen as providing different sorts of assistance at different stages . . .' (Reynolds *et al.*, 2005: 10).

The following list of external partner roles and responsibilities was aggregated from data collected from forty-three academic partners (Ewing *et al.*, 2004) who had all participated in the same system-wide action learning project, across fifty projects, in over a hundred schools. It was felt that academic partners needed to:

- facilitate;
- bring a fresh perspective on teachers' practice;
- validate teachers' practice;
- be a sounding board;
- respond to particular issues and provide feedback;
- listen;
- provide resources;
- advise and guide;
- expose teachers to new ideas;
- generally assist;
- clarify;
- be a critical friend;
- provide input;
- stimulate teacher discussion; and
- extend teacher thinking.

This list certainly supports Reynold *et al.*'s (2005) comments about the diversity they independently and as a group perceived in their roles. It also demonstrates that sometimes one role may be partly contradictory to or in tension with another.

In our view, mutual benefits for both the school team members and the external partner are important, so that the relationship is one of equality. The benefits from the perspective of the external partner have not yet been adequately explored. It is clear that working with schools certainly allows academic partners to maintain their credibility and establish authentic partnerships that can be mutually beneficial and potentially provide a springboard for other initiatives. Joint presentations about the knowledge created and understandings developed from the action learning process can be important outcomes. Several comments from academic partners suggest this can be the case:

> When you work with a school community by necessity it involves many hours of negotiation and communication if this kind of project is to be successful. I have tried to maximise this learning opportunity for myself and have remained involved with the team at conference level.
>
> (Ewing *et al.*, 2004: 92)

In terms of my own teaching there has been a spin-off. I now have teachers from the action learning team involved in working with my pre-service teachers.

(Ewing *et al.*, 2004: 92)

Intellectual property issues will also need discussion and resolution if a publication is to be an outcome of the process.

Scaffolds for working productively

Some action learning teams find the reflection phases most challenging. Critical friends may be able to develop scaffolds to facilitate the reflection process. Below are two examples of scaffolds developed by an academic partner, David Smith, for use with school action learning teams. The first (Figure 6.1) was designed to assist individual team members to reflect after one cycle of action learning and before a team reflective discussion. The second (Figure 6.2) was used to assist individual teachers and then teams to plan a cycle of action learning. These processes also provided some valuable evidence for team members of their own learning, as discussed in Chapter 3, 'Enabling action learning'.

---

1. What are the three most important increases in your understanding of the elements of the quality teaching framework?

2. What are the three most important things that you have learnt about applying elements of the framework to your classes?

3. What are the most important things that you have learnt about action learning as a strategy for teacher professional learning?

4. What do you still need to learn about action learning to make it more effective in the next cycle?

Figure 6.1 Reflecting scaffold

(Smith, 2008a)

Planning for team action learning
This scaffold has been developed to assist you in planning your action learning activities during 2008 focused on teaching and assessment practices for quality teaching and student learning. It is designed both for reflection and completion by teachers individually initially and then as a basis for sharing in pairs or threes towards decisions for each of the three action learning cycles.

Reflection/evaluation
Identify the elements that you would like to work with in your own teaching practice. These may be those you think you already emphasise in your teaching and assessment practices and you may wish to gain evidence to confirm those perceptions. Alternatively they may be those you would like to improve.

Decisions for further action: big picture
Considering the elements you have identified, write down the learning outcomes related to your own teaching practice that you would like to achieve by the end of term 4. Keep in mind what is achievable within the limited time available.

Decisions for further action: small steps
Consider what you have planned to teach in term 2. What activity will you engage in for cycle 1 during your release time in term 2 (e.g. backward mapping; modifying previous planned unit plans or assessment tasks; planning a learning activity with a colleague...)?

What resources will you need?

What role will your teacher partner play?

What evidence will you collect?

Anticipated outcomes for yourself?

your students?

Strategies to share your learning with other teachers in the school?

Figure 6.2 Planning scaffold

(Adapted from Smith, 2007)

Conclusion

Thus, the role of the external partner can be daunting and should not to be approached or undertaken lightly. Roland Barthes (1982) once talked about a 'collegial sandpit'. This metaphor seems appropriate when conceptualising the challenging role of the external partner as a critical friend in an action learning process. They must multitask. Initially, they must establish a relationship of reciprocity with the action learning team to allow knowledge arising from the action learning process to be co-created, rather than imposed from outside or above. They must also be flexible to be able to move between a number of different roles and responsibilities as required. This includes shaping and framing ideas, validating teacher knowledge and perspectives, guiding the action learning process where necessary, confronting stereotypes, reflecting ideas back to the team, monitoring their own learning, providing feedback and always ensuring that the school team is in control of the process. All of these aspects must be undertaken within the politics of a particular school culture and history. Yet, equally valuable are the benefits to the external partner themselves, although these are not always clearly understood or articulated. In the future, the notion of reciprocity needs to be explored further in teasing out the relationship between school action learning sets or teams and their external partner or critical friend.

The next chapter considers the gathering of evidence and how we can learn from that evidence.

Chapter 7

Gathering and learning from evidence

Action learning depends on learning through professional conversation. The basis for decision-making in action learning teams can be shifted to more robust ways of thinking by seeking evidence to answer questions such as: What is the problem? How might we address this? How might we improve? What is happening here? What intervention might we try? How do we know the intervention is working? What can we use to inform our professional judgements? Central to each of these questions are enquiry, action and reflection. This chapter explores the ways in which teachers gather evidence in action learning, as well as how it is used to inform professional conversations and to promote innovation. We discuss options such as peer observation, the selection and use of instruments, focus groups, reflection, reporting, capturing episodes and the role of professional sharing. While the chapter acknowledges the roles each of these tools plays in research, it focuses on the part they play and what it means to engage in learning with colleagues from collaborative reflection and analysis, as part of the action learning process.

Practical wisdom

In education, a distinction is sometimes drawn between two types of knowledge: practical wisdom and generalisable, research-based knowledge (Korthagen *et al.*, 2001). Action learning deals with local situations, their practices, their people and their community. It deals with questions such as: What works here? Will this practice improve things? And, what do I do about this here and now? The point of emphasis in action learning is on the use and development of practical wisdom to make well-informed decisions. Practical wisdom has been described by Berlin as:

A sense of what will 'work' and what will not. It is a capacity, in the first place for synthesis rather than analysis, for knowledge in the sense that trainers know their animals, or parents their children, or conductors their orchestras . . . above all it is an acute sense of what fits with what, what springs from what, what leads to what; how things seem to vary to different observers, what the effects of such an experience on them may be; what the result is likely to be in a concrete situation or interplay of human beings and impersonal forces.

(cited in Hargreaves, 2007a: 48)

The prominence of practical wisdom does not deny the importance of other sources of knowledge and practices. In all cases of action learning we have studied, action learning has been influenced by a research knowledge base that teachers have gained access to through a variety of sources, including: higher education courses, professional associations, text-based sources, professional development programmes or external consultants. Practical wisdom, however, plays a role in determining what information is shared; what knowledge is selected initially as worth using; deciding which of a variety of pedagogies might work in a school; and choosing which strategies or practices to try out. Hargreaves (2007b) elaborates on the interplay in education between practical wisdom and the research knowledge base by comparing the role of the teacher with that of a doctor in general practice. Specifically, for doctors there is an extensive knowledge base about the maintenance of good health, diagnosis and treatment of disease, but practical wisdom underpins decision-making in dealing with individual patients, and this is informed by the doctor's knowledge of the individual and his/her circumstances. Similarly, for teachers there is a knowledge base available, but it is less rich and less certain. There is, therefore, a greater and more fundamental dependence on practical wisdom in the teaching profession.

The practical wisdom of teachers has often been criticised because it is inherently in danger of being a rigid, practical mythology – a captive of mores, lore and ritual. Cox, for example, claims that there are four grounds that teachers use to justify their practices:

- tradition (how it has always been done);
- prejudice (how I like it done);
- dogma (this is the 'right' way to do it; and
- ideology (as required by the current orthodoxy) (cited in Hargreaves, 2007b: 12).

Teachers' dependence on practical wisdom means that this wisdom needs to be laid open to scrutiny, open to revision and to learning. It is here that action learning plays an important role, as it permits the synthesis of richly contextualised knowledge. However, if teachers are to have confidence in this knowledge, it needs to be underpinned by local evidence and local experience.

Experience as evidence

The complexity of teaching means that there are no certain ways to go about education (Hammersley, 2007). Because of this uncertainty, 'there remains the expectation that teachers are required to be reflective and self-evaluative; in short to learn from experience' (Turner and Bash, 1999: 135). This requires reflection on experience (as outlined in detail in the chapter on 'The dynamics of action learning') as an essential process in action learning:

> [Reflection] helps teachers to make wise and principled decisions. It is about developing teachers' self-knowledge, the ability to see through teaching situations and understand the meaning of what is happening in their classroom and school.
>
> (Ghaye and Ghaye, 1998: 3)

Pertinent to this chapter is what experiences and evidence feed into this reflection. At this point, it is important to accept that there are no objective data on teaching and learning because, no matter how we select and obtain information, it is in some way distorted by the process (Kemmis, 2007). In school the teacher is the centre of a feedback loop that sustains the teaching–learning system. The capacity of the teacher to analyse and interpret the situation, to select and give meaning to the data and information, is critical to the synthesis of an understanding of what is happening, what is needed and what might be done. The teacher is the human instrument gathering data and sifting through them to determine what ought to be done. In action learning, this process is refined, extended, made explicit, shared and scrutinised.

Action learning often begins with a concern that is stimulated by reflection on the current situation. The concern is grounded in evidence: events, episodes and trends that are discerned by the teachers, school executive or sometimes a central authority. The experiences or information may include such things as classroom experiences, student behaviours, student assessment results, truancy levels, identification of disadvantaged groups, falling enrolments, dissatisfaction with current pedagogy or practice, or opportunities provided by a new technology. Whatever the initial concern, it may give rise to an analysis of the current situation, including its current activities and practices; social relationships and organisational structures and procedures; and discourse and communication (Cooper and Boyd, 1994).

Once the concern is identified and the goal determined, there is a need to match the evidence gathered to the improvement sought, as well as to decide what evidence will inform the ongoing reflection and contribute to teacher learning. It is not possible here to outline the many forms of evidence teachers gather in action learning, but some examples will serve to illustrate important features of well-informed action learning. The intention is for us to discuss the role in learning of modes of evidence gathering and the consequent synthesis of knowledge. However, this is not intended to devalue teachers' 'informal and routine daily information processing' (Burton and Bartlett, 2005: 14); the ad hoc sharing of experience and the professional talk associated with this is essential in free-wheeling, more serendipitous forms of action learning.

Process or product?

When schools or teachers engage in action learning, it is because they want something to improve or they want to be able to do something better. Because action learning is located in the workplace, the learning is inextricably linked with practice, and typically the outcomes sought include student learning outcomes. The emphasis on teacher and student learning as outcomes to be achieved through action learning varies in different settings. This means that the type of evidence gathered to inform the action learning also varies. In broad terms, there are often two types of things teachers want to get evidence about: the outcome and the process.

Outcomes may be relatively specific: for example, we may want to know whether the students improved their numeracy; developed more informed views about environmental issues; or became more engaged learners. Similarly, a group of teachers may want to determine whether they themselves have learnt something, such as more about what numeracy means for their students; or understood the circumstances of disadvantaged students in their classes. Teachers may also identify in advance that they want to know how to use a teaching strategy, such as cooperative group work, as an outcome of the action learning. The goal may be to learn about a particular pedagogy, a specific teaching strategy, and to implement a set of practices. On the other hand, the outcome might be relatively open-ended, in that the teachers may commit to an action learning group to discuss practices and ideas about teaching and learning in anticipation that this will lead to professional learning that is yet to be determined. All of these outcomes beg the question: How will we know whether improvement has occurred? For example, has numeracy improved? Are our students more engaged? Does our group of teachers better understand the new pedagogy and its related practices? What have we learnt from the sharing of ideas? Implicit in these questions is the requirement to gather data and evidence.

The phrasing of these questions suggests that we want to know about a change in achievement, either periodically during the action learning process, or before and after the implementation of an action. For example, students' literacy could be tested before and after an action is implemented, with the scores used as evidence about whether the action has improved literacy learning. However, one problem with such before and after testing is that it does not yield information about the process that led to the improvement. Also, in schools where action learning is occurring, many things are happening and many changes are taking place, and it is very difficult to attribute any improvement to a specific cause. So, while the growing emphasis on accountability has resulted in tests becoming an important feature in much of the action learning we have observed in schools, they do not provide insight into the process or how the improvements in learning came about in complex classroom environments.

The following sections of the chapter consider specific forms of evidence gathering in action learning. These are not intended as a comprehensive list. Rather, they serve as indications of the types of evidence gathering that some teachers have found useful.

High-stakes tests

In many of the action learning projects we have studied, high-stakes external tests have been influential (Aubusson *et al.*, 2006; Ewing *et al.*, 2005). They often provide valuable feedback, which can be taken as an indicator of the success of projects and practices implemented as part of action learning processes. It has been commonplace for teachers and team leaders to cite basic skills tests of literacy or numeracy as indicators of success during or following changes in school practices. The tests can be useful in 'convincing' parents, teachers and administrators that the work of the action learning team has led to improvements, which can help gain support for new or continued projects, as well as the action learning process per se. For example, in Sundew Elementary School, improved results in the literacy basic skills test following an extended intervention in literacy was used to 'sell' the idea of similar action learning targeting student numeracy. The apparent success associated with the literacy intervention promoted participation among staff in the numeracy project, gleaned support from the school executive and won the backing of parents (Aubusson *et al.*, 2006). It has been argued that success in such high-stakes testing is the most important indicator of school improvement and, by implication, it is critical in determining the success of school-based professional learning and its initiatives (DuFour, 2004). The significance of such tests is impossible to disregard. As broad indicators of progress they are valuable, and their detailed analysis can be very productive in identifying strengths, weaknesses and aspects of learning that require particular attention in future teaching. Indeed, in many instances of action learning, the high-stakes tests have been used to identify areas teachers want to target in their action learning. But, in part, because these tests are very infrequent, they do not provide the timely feedback essential for the progressive refinement of the iterative process that is action learning. Hence, in this chapter we also need to look at other forms of evidence.

Peer observation

Peer observation is another form of evidence gathering that can be used to inform action learning. Peer observation is not for everyone. It is a double-edged sword, because some teachers find it threatening and may withdraw from action learning where it is proposed (Aubusson *et al.,* 2007). On the other hand, it can stimulate rich, professional conversations based on shared experience (Schuck *et al.,* 2008). Peer observation is particularly appropriate when the aim is to develop a deeper understanding of current or new pedagogy in order to improve teaching practice. Classroom observation can take many forms, including moment-by-moment recording on an inventory by a researcher; inspection by supervisors to judge or advise on practice; or observation by an inexperienced teacher of a more 'expert' teacher to learn from seeing teaching in action. But here, peer observation is distinguished from these other forms because the observer and observed are peers, equals in the process, even if they may occupy unequal positions elsewhere in the school. For example, a head teacher may observe teachers in their department, but it needs to be understood that the different positions of rank are irrelevant or suspended during the peer observation. On a pragmatic note, it has often proved helpful for the more experienced or 'higher-ranked' teachers to be the first to be observed by others. The process requires the development of trust, including agreed confidentiality about what can and cannot be discussed with others.

Peer observation in action learning works best when the aim is to generate professional conversation. This professional conversation is informed and stimulated by the observation. The nature of the observation may take a variety of forms. The aim is not to record every detail, otherwise a video camera or audio recoding would be used. Peer observation is less objective and it works well for this reason. In part, its success is a result of the observer being a teacher who can make decisions about what is important. Observations are selective and may be idiosyncratic. This selectivity helps to focus the ensuing discussion and allows peers to see what others view as salient in teaching.

Instruments used in peer observation vary enormously. The observer may use a blank page and aim to provide a record of events, such as samples of teacher–student talk, either with or without their own comments and reflections. Alternatively, the observer may use an observation schedule with a checklist or a guiding set of questions. Some examples are shown below.

Observations without comment – a verbatim record from an event

TEACHER: Give me that magazine.

STUDENT: I'll put it away. (Student begins to put magazine in bag)

TEACHER: You had your chance. (Walking towards student) Give it to me now.

STUDENT: (Starts to put magazine in bag)

TEACHER: I want that magazine.

STUDENT: (Continues to put magazine in bag) Come on Miss it's gone, what's the problem? You should buy one if you want it.

CLASS: (Laughter)

(Unpublished observation notes)

The observation of this incident resulted in a conversation about how to deal with such behaviour and how to avoid confrontation and escalation. The notes resulted from an unguided observation.

Observations with comments and later reflection

The record below includes initial observation notes and records from later conversations and reflections.

> . . . Like me you seem to carry most of the argument. How can I get them to carry most of the argument? Too much for 2 hours? Do they need to operate as a collective for the whole 2 hours? There is so much here that is so rich. Are you getting all the learning you want from the experiences you provide?
>
> (Initial note made during observation.)

Later reflection after professional conversation:

> Why does John feel so much more comfortable about allowing students to experience his rich tasks and then not join the dots? I so have to join the dots for them (my students) for fear – fear that they may not get it. I realise I speak to them about letting go of control and allowing students to learn for themselves, base their ideas on evidence and critical appraisal – but I don't trust them. I almost always have to join the dots. I know what the point is and I just can't resist. Making sure they get it. How? – By telling them. And just how exactly does this make sure they get it? – Better that I let them get it themselves. Better that I try to have them remain provoked and curious – wanting. Here is the difference! John trusts his students – I do not!
>
> (Transcript extract from Aubusson *et al.*, 2008)

Comments provided in this way often reveal thinking about teaching and learning. They provide insights into the observer's views of his/her own teaching, stimulate professional conversation and enable learning for both the observer and the observed. The evidence is not so much about the lesson per se but rather about the practical wisdom of the observer and observed, which is sometimes taken for granted.

Observations guided by a schedule checklist

The observation guide below provides a list of features that are associated with 'productive pedagogy'. The observer rates each item on a 1–5 scale to indicate the extent to which these features are manifested in the observed lesson. The extract lists three of the many features related to having a supportive classroom environment that are associated with productive pedagogy.

Table 7.1 Extract from a productive pedagogy observation checklist*

Feature	Description	Score
Social support	Social support is characterised by an atmosphere of mutual respect and support between teacher and students, and among students.	4
Academic	Students are engaged and on task. They show enthusiasm for their work by raising questions, contributing to group activities and helping peers.	2
Explicit quality performance criteria	The criteria for judging the range of student performance are made explicit. Using tools such as rubrics.	I
Self-regulation	The direction of student behaviour is implicit and self-regulatory.	3

* Such checklists often include fifteen to twenty items.
(Adapted from www.decs.sa.gov.au/ned/files/links/Prod_Ped_Checklist.doc)

One of the difficulties with such ratings schemes is that teachers often feel judged by the 'score'. However, the checklist aims to create greater understanding of what is happening in the classroom and to promote teacher talk about the pedagogy. In short, the aim is to learn more about productive pedagogy and how to use it to improve practice. Critical to this is the recognition that a score of 1 is not necessarily 'bad', because such a score might be entirely appropriate in a particular lesson. On the other hand, consistently low ratings on an item may flag a cause for concern. Additionally, changes in ratings, whether up or down, over a series of lessons, may provide some indication about the effectiveness of a teaching intervention that the action learning team is attempting. It is worth stressing here that the learning from the observation checklist does not come from a determination of the score alone, but from the conversation among peers about the lesson that arises from this evidence gathered about the lesson.

Focus groups

Focus groups of students, teachers or parents can often provide useful feedback about progress on innovations applied as part of the action learning process. They can also offer valuable insights early in the action learning process by identifying concerns, problems and needs. Much could be said about the selection of focus groups, which may typically be random, or purposeful. As a considerable amount of time and effort is invested in creating, running and reporting on focus groups, it is wise to select the group purposefully. Certainly, there is little to be gained in the action learning context by inviting a student or parent to participate in a focus group when he or she is known to be uninterested or unlikely to contribute. We suggest that the nature of the activities and goals of the action learning should guide the constituency of the focus groups. For example, if a goal includes increasing community engagement or parental involvement with the school, it makes sense for the focus group to include representatives from various relevant parts of the community and parent body. Similarly, if an aim is to improve outcomes for all students, then the focus group needs to be broadly representative. By contrast, if the goals relate primarily to a subgroup of students, such as low-achieving students or gifted and talented students, or early career teachers, then the focus groups would target these.

Focus groups can be conducted effectively by teachers in their own schools. There is often concern, however, that students and parents may not feel free to speak openly and frankly, to voice concerns or to criticise under these circumstances. Therefore, it is advantageous to have someone from outside the school conduct and report findings from focus groups, even if teachers also conduct some focus groups themselves.

In a study of action learning in a science faculty, there was an external partner/consultant-researcher who conducted focus groups with students (Hoban et al., 1997). The partner sought information about their experiences in lessons and then provided verbatim extracts and audio recordings from focus groups about, among other things, what students thought were good and bad teaching and learning. This focus group information provided important feedback, which guided the action learning in the school. Significantly, the external partner had great freedom in determining what would be discussed in the focus groups. In this case, the outsider not only provided an environment in which students could speak openly, but also brought new perspectives to the gathering and interpretation of evidence about the school-based initiative. It would be interesting to speculate on how the successful action learning might have been constrained if the school action learning set had exerted greater control over what information should be sought in the focus groups.

In another project, a team of head teachers from five schools were working together to increase student engagement with science (Aubusson and Griffin, 2008). One of the team's initiatives was the introduction of a research project carried out by students in groups and reported as an extensive 'Science–Techno Museum' display. Two partner consultant-researchers conducted focus groups with both teachers and students in all five schools to determine what had been achieved and how it might be improved. The focus groups provided an opportunity for feedback on all aspects of the initiative, including perceptions of the learning that had occurred; strengths and weaknesses of the initiative; matters that had facilitated and inhibited the initiative; and indications of student interest and engagement. The following guiding questions were used, which might be adapted for use in many focus groups to gather information for action learning:

- Do you think the project was worthwhile?
- What do you think you learnt from it?
- What do you think helped?
- What things do you think hindered it?
- Would you recommend that this or something like it be done again?
- What advice would you give to students or teachers if something similar were done again?

In a focus group, it is common that short or glib responses to questions can dominate discussions. If such responses are all that is sought, a survey may be more productive. It is important that focus groups seek richer information. To achieve this, responses to these questions were followed up by further probing questions such as:

- What makes you say that?
- Can you give me an example of . . .?
- The other group suggested . . . do you agree? Why?
- If that was not helpful can you think of a better way to do it?
- One thing we were thinking of doing next term is . . . do you think that is a good idea? How would you change that? Etc.

In the case of the Science–Techno Museum project, the focus groups supplied strong indications that the initiative had been successful in promoting student interest and involvement in science learning. They also revealed that the Science–Techno Museum was well regarded by students and teachers alike. Conversely, they also indicated that the project had resulted in excessive workloads for teachers; confusion about expectations among some students; and reservations about some of the support materials used to guide the process. As a result of this evidence gathering, the action learning team of head teachers was provided with recommendations from teachers, students and consultants that could be used to improve this initiative if it was repeated in the future. Significantly, in the context of action learning, the focus group report stimulated professional discussions and learning about factors influencing students' motivation and engagement in science.

Just as teachers and external consultants can conduct focus groups, it is also useful to involve students in the process by encouraging students to gather information themselves in focus group meetings with their peers. Students can be extensively and productively involved in gathering data to inform professional learning and school change (Groundwater-Smith and Mockler, 2002). This involvement not only provides evidence from the students' perspective, but also invites students to play an active and influential role in decision-making in their school.

Capturing experiences, stories and anecdotes

It is notoriously difficult to capture what is happening in a classroom, but classroom experiences, stories and anecdotes are another form of evidence that can be used in action learning. The stories that teachers tell about their authentic classroom experience are often powerful and evocative for other teachers:

> Stories can help us to understand by making the abstract concrete and accessible. What is only dimly perceived at the level of principle may become vivid and affectively powerful in the concrete. Further, stories motivate us. Even that which we understand at the abstract level may not move us to action, whereas story often does.
>
> (Noddings and Witherell, 1991: 279–80)

It is difficult to gather evidence about teachers' classroom experiences, as a small proportion of teachers use written records of classroom events. However, the most common way in which teachers share teaching episodes and events is by recounting recollections using anecdotes. It would be difficult to overstate the importance of these anecdotes in teachers' professional conversations or their influence in decision-making processes. However, the management of these conversations in an action learning context requires an able team leader and a well-focused set to ensure the shared stories form the basis for productive, reflective analysis. Some questions to guide such sharing could include:

- Why am I sharing this anecdote?
- Will it contribute to my learning or that of others?
- What contextual information is needed to allow people to make sense of how the episode came to happen?
- In what ways did the student, teacher or environment contribute to the making of this episode?
- If the anecdote identifies good practice, what did the teacher do that contributed to this 'good' outcome? What might I be able to do to achieve something similar?
- If this raises a concern or problem, what contributed to the problem? What actions might alleviate or resolve the problem?

Anecdotes can provide insights into developments and learning that may be difficult to capture in any other way. For example, at Blue Wren Elementary School, a teacher was asked about evidence of the positive effects of what she was doing in her class as part of the school's action learning process. She responded by saying with assurance that it had but she had 'no hard evidence' of it. When pressed for a third time, another teacher said 'What about Mike?', at which point the teacher told a story about Mike, a child with 'behaviour and learning problems', who, after visiting a circus, wrote three sentences about it. 'The grammar and spelling were terrible', she explained, but, having previously not written recounts, it was remarkable that he wrote three sentences. This provided evidence that Mike was making progress, although this would be very unlikely to be shown in many forms of testing or assessment. This story evidence was very impressive to other teachers who knew Mike and others like him in the class. It provided a description of similar encounters other teachers had experienced with Mike, adding to the tapestry of 'lived experience' (van Manen, 1992) that informed the teachers about their action learning. But the evidence was not in the artefact per se, the three lines of writing, it was in the history and context, which required a story for its explication.

Video evidence can also provide a useful source of information about experiences of teaching and learning for discussion in action learning teams. One advantage of video is that the teacher can choose the part of the lesson he or she wants to share. Some teachers are even using mobile phones to record short dialogues, photograph events and record teacher or student actions (Fogwill and Aubusson, 2006). For example, one teacher used his mobile phone to record short dialogues and video and photograph role-playing in his physics class. Students found it relatively unobtrusive and regarded its use as normal in their life experience. The recordings were short and easily shared with those at the school taking an interest in his teaching ideas. Nevertheless, recollections of experiences remain the most common form of evidence, even in a world where a plethora of devices exists to digitally capture events.

Reflective records

The role of reflection is a recurring theme in this book, and there are few tools for teacher learning about which more has been written. Here, the emphasis is on reflective accounts as a source of evidence in action learning, and there is only space to consider a few examples. In broad terms, reflective records can be entirely open-ended, unfettered writing about almost anything related to the concern being addressed, the professional learning as it occurs, or the educational goal being pursued. Such reflections are often stimulated by a critical event and may include a description of the episode and the thinking it stimulates. Reflective records are often guided by a scaffold of questions. At Azure Bay Elementary School, all the teachers of each year group taught using one identical activity each week. To promote thinking about this activity, all the teachers agreed to keep a daily reflective journal, with the following guiding questions:

• What happened?
• What was successful and what was not?

- What assumptions underpin my thinking about this event?
- What might I do differently next time?
- What have I learnt from this?

These reflections then fed into regular discussions among teachers about the teaching and learning in their classes. Periodic reflections can also be used to provide information about the progress of the action learning process itself. For example, teachers in six schools used a scaffold on three scales (adapted from Sheffield *et al.*, 2004) to review and reflect on their progress with action learning itself. Part of the adapted scaffold, the utilisation scale, is shown below.

- I see myself as:

    Drop-out – I have not continued with the innovation after the first attempt.
    Struggler – I am using things mechanically, just doing what I'm told.
    Domesticator – I used the new ideas successfully but adapted them to fit my normal approach.
    Succeedor – I've changed what I do but I am still very dependent on support.
    Innovator – I understand the innovation, use and vary it as part of my teaching.

- What helped me reach or brought me to this?
- How might I progress further?
- What is influencing my professional learning?

(Aubusson *et al.*, 2006)

This scaffold was quite confronting and provocative in its use of labels. As with peer observation instruments, discussed above, it may not be the label one chooses that is important, but rather the way it challenges the way we see ourselves when we reject, adopt, adapt or innovate our practice.

Reflective accounts can serve as ways to reveal teachers' perceptions about whether, in their professional judgement, a practice is helping to improve student learning. They serve to provide insights into the thinking that is guiding what teachers do, what influences their teaching, why they teach, and who they are as professionals. The 'onion model', so called because of its layers of deeper reflection, has been used in the Netherlands to help teachers explore deeper personal qualities that influence them (Korthagen and Vasalos, 2005). The model begins with reflection on the situation or environment and progresses through a sequence of six layers to consider one's underlying mission:

1   Environment – What do I encounter? What am I dealing with?
2   Behaviour – What do I do?

3   Competencies – What am I competent at?
4   Beliefs – What do I believe?
5   Identity – Who am I in my work?
6   Mission – What inspires me?

(Korthagen and Vasalos, 2005)

By exposing underlying perceptions, beliefs and thinking, teachers are open to critique and change. Reflective records provide valuable data about processes being trialled in action learning. They also provide data about the thinking that underpins action and an opportunity to examine assumptions. For this reason, reflection in action learning usually occurs in two phases. First, the teacher reflects on actions soon after an event. Then later, the action learning team or teacher revisits these initial reflective records, or provides an oral commentary on the initial reflection. This extends the process to what is sometimes called collaborative reflection or reflective conversations. Such productive collaborative reflections are characterised by the following: consideration of values; making the private public; looking back to look forward; making sense of teaching learning experiences; and interrogation of experiences and assumptions (Ghaye and Ghaye, 1998). Robust collaborative conversations are not for the faint hearted, but they can play an important role in the action learning set's synthesis of professional knowledge.

Work samples

The work students do and the products they create are important indicators of their progress and can be used as evidence in action learning. When teachers are seeking an improvement in their students' learning, it is unsurprising that they will talk about the quality of the work their students produce. We see this in that reports from teachers, about how things are going in their classes, are often littered with anecdotes about students' work. In action learning, it is useful to collect work samples to share with others. These can provide a source of evidence about how innovations and strategies employed by the team are progressing.

When collecting work samples, it is important both to ensure that samples relevant to the action learning goals are collected, and also to remain open to any unanticipated outcomes that might be evident in their work. For example, in an action learning project that aimed to improve literacy among students from diverse cultural backgrounds in Staghorn Elementary School, the teachers decided to provide rich contextual opportunities for writing and to combine writing with other modes of artistic communication, such as painting and photographs. One of the activities encouraged students to interview older family members to learn more about their origins. The projects that students produced showed that they were willing to write more extensively than in most previous tasks. While the aim of the project was to improve literacy, the work samples also suggested there was pride in their family origins; a willingness to share information about their cultural heritage; and significant parental involvement in students' learning. Teacher comments at meetings also indicted that many children seemed to have developed enhanced self-esteem. It was noted that some students who almost never did any work outside the classroom or rarely completed assigned tasks had completed this task, with some of it accomplished outside normal class time. This was only one of many activities that the action learning team had initiated in the school, and there is no suggestion that this activity alone produced the outcomes identified. But it was an indication that the initiatives of the action learning set at the school were producing positive outcomes, some of which were manifested in the work samples. Some of the outcomes were intended, and others were inadvertent. Some work samples were brought to action learning meetings and were influential in the ongoing future strategies proposed by the action learning set.

Often, work samples are collected after new strategies have begun and when different types of activity are tried with students. It is useful to collect samples before trying out new practices, as these can provide some baseline information about current student achievements, which can be used for comparisons with work samples that are collected as the action learning process proceeds. In addition, it is our view that work samples provide not only evidence of achievement but also opportunities for concrete displays to celebrate successes.

School and class records

Schools maintain many records that can inform action learning. At a high school with a student population drawn from an area of low socio-economic status, teachers and executives were concerned that students were becoming disillusioned with education, exhibiting disruptive behaviour and disengaging from school during their first year of high school (Gonczi and Riordan, 2002). In this school, they formed a team of teachers keen to work together to address these problems. They met regularly to discuss and implement a variety of strategies to reduce the seemingly harmful effects of the current students' transition to high school. As is typical of action learning, the strategies employed were varied. They included: one teacher teaching many subjects, so that the teaching and relationship between teacher and student were more like those of their elementary school experience; changes to the orientation programme; and more extensive exchange of information between the feeder primary schools and this high school. An important source of data in this case was school and class records. Specifically, they found that there was a decrease in: absences from class, truancy, suspensions and expulsions. Furthermore, not only were these rates lower than in previous years at the school, but they were also lower than those of nearby schools that comprised students of similar socio-economic backgrounds. In developing an action learning evidentiary plan, the set should consider what is already available in the school that can inform the process.

From practical wisdom to professional knowledge

Action learning is professional learning that, among other things, can involve teachers considering evidence related to their school, themselves and their students. The processes of gathering evidence, analysing information and the cooperative synthesis of knowledge that underpin these activities can vary, from ad hoc recollections shared at occasional team meetings to use of highly sophisticated instruments in collaborative enquiry. If teaching is to move from a system and practices that are informed by practical wisdom to education that is built on a foundation of professional knowledge, then evidence must play a significant role in the production of this knowledge (Groundwater-Smith and Mockler, 2007). It is the rigorous discussion of evidence at team meetings that confirms or disconfirms practical wisdom and provides a bridge to professional knowledge. Much of the knowledge cannot be established empirically and derived in controlled conditions. Rather, it is more often refined or created locally, where particular contexts and circumstances of schools can be taken into account. Thus, action learning as professional learning can be enhanced by evidence that may be argued and debated in determining principles and practices that teachers and the broader community can trust.

As a learning process, action learning is often less widely reported than school-based research, but its progress and outcomes are often extensively reported in the school community. It is not often reported where the participants – teachers, students, parents – are well known and where the information may cause harm or influence the way people are viewed in this community. The ethics of gathering evidence, sharing information and reporting in action learning are discussed in detail in the next chapter: 'Ethical action learning'.

Chapter 8

Ethical action learning

> The moral responsibility of the school, and of those who conduct it, is to society . . . The educational system which does not recognise that this fact entails upon it an ethical responsibility is derelict and a defaulter. It is not doing what it was called into existence to do, and what it pretends to do. Hence the entire structure of the school in general and its concrete workings in particular need to be considered from time to time with reference to the social position and function of the school.
>
> (Dewey, 1909, republished in 1975: 7–8)

Dewey's quote reminds us that, at all times, schools need to be both socially and morally competent organisations. Nearly a century later, Campbell (2003) asserts that ethics must always be a primary framework when thinking about teachers and their work. This means teachers must consider and protect the rights of others and think through the consequences of their actions, so that they are not likely to bring harm to others, intentionally or unintentionally. It is somewhat difficult to define and measure ethical processes in organisations such as schools, but this does not mean we should avoid the challenge to ensure that we 'do the right thing' ethically. Moral principles should also underpin any action learning relationships or actions arising through action learning. As Revans (1983a: 41–2) wrote: 'those responsible for handling change must therefore be able to formulate *and support by personal example*' (our emphasis).

Professional learning, like all learning, needs to occur within 'an ethical culture that pursues fairness, respect for difference, doing the right thing, trust and other aspects of good social and organisational cultures' (Cox, 2003: 16). Teachers involved in action learning must apply their capacity to facilitate an ethical awareness, both about their teaching and towards their students, to their awareness about their own professional learning practices (Hartog, 2004). The all-encompassing and earnest ethical mantra, 'do no harm', needs to be carefully unpacked in action learning contexts.

Throughout this book we have emphasised that the processes that encapsulate action learning can lead to positive change in schools, when owned and led by teachers. For these processes to operate effectively in any organisation, and especially in schools, it is critical that ethical practices are observed. Yet to date there appears to have been little time or energy devoted to thinking explicitly about ethical action learning. For example, as the group discussions in action learning get personal and explicit, teachers should be careful to keep the sharing on a professional level and not be tempted to become personally critical of other teachers or executives in the school. This chapter draws heavily on established principles about ethics from research and evaluation literature, particularly practitioner research literature, to provide an introduction to the discussion of ethical action learning. In doing this, we invite further research in the field and suggest a number of imperatives that are crucial for ethical action learning in schools.

Action learning requires us to break from the 'saturated consciousness' (Apple, 1990: 3) and the rituals and constraints of professional practice to ask big questions in a collaborative context, in order to address dilemmas and issues that may ultimately lead to change. This collaborative nature of action learning means that some principles immediately assume prominence in any discussion of ethics. While acknowledging that action learning and action research are different (as elaborated in Chapter 1), the collaborative processes of the two for school-based change are similar. To this end, we have adapted the 'over-riding ethical guidelines' proposed for practitioner research by Groundwater-Smith and Mockler (2007: 205). These guidelines, which include trust, confidentiality, genuine collaboration, transparency and accountability, seem to be of most relevance to action learning. Each aspect of the guidelines is explored briefly below and must be considered in relation to three aspects of action learning relationships in schools: internal relationships between members of the action learning team; the relationships between the action learning team and those outside it; and the relationship between the action learning team and the external facilitator.

Trust and confidentiality

Trust and confidentiality are important and essential ethical principles in action learning. An action learning team will not function effectively if the participants do not trust each other. In fact, trust is probably the single most important factor in achieving a successful action learning process. Based on a report on six case study schools in the Sydney Catholic Education Diocese, where action learning projects were focused on improving students' literacy and numeracy outcomes, Smith notes that the depth and complexity of professional conversations depend on the levels of trust, honesty and risk that have been established between members of these action learning sets (Smith, 2008b).

As well as being able to trust other group members, each action learning participant must be trustworthy (Mishler, 1990). All members of the action learning team must be able to trust each other and be trusted so that real sharing can occur.

Therefore, as elaborated in Chapters 2 and 3, a group that has been formed for the first time may need to take some time to develop trusting relationships before the action learning process can proceed further. From the outset, team members need to be fully informed about what is expected. They must have opportunities to ask questions and identify any concerns they may have about the process. As the action learning process unfolds, participants need to feel confident about revisiting expectations or raising new issues, especially when they feel uncomfortable or challenged. In fact, as teachers become more honest in their action learning meetings, they may expose their personal vulnerabilities as practitioners. Teachers, like everyone else, are better at discussing their strengths rather than their weaknesses. But it is a sign of a maturing professional learning culture when teachers can share their strengths and weaknesses with others in the action learning set or group, with the expectation that they will receive suggestions for improvement. Everyone needs to feel confident that sharing their concerns in an open and honest manner is their right and that their privacy and confidences will be respected.

Here it is worth considering the question posed by Griffith (2003: 101) regarding whether one person's cooperation and consensus can be another's coercion and constraint. From the beginning of the action learning process, it is important for team members to understand that it is their choice to continue to be involved in the process and that they are free to withdraw if they feel uncomfortable, or alternatively, unable to make the commitment to the process.

Genuine collaboration

If mutuality, honour and respect are foregrounded (Groundwater-Smith and Mockler, 2007: 10) as important attributes of an ethical process and implemented from the beginning of the action learning process in a school, collaboration is more likely to be genuine, rather than contrived (Hargreaves, 1994). There may be times when issues or actions that arise from the process need to be cross-checked (Altrichter *et al.*, 1993) during group meetings. Some agreement will also need to be reached about how conflict will be managed. In fact, the group is likely to mature if they are prepared to share and work through conflict. Perhaps consensus will be reached, but this is not always the case. If not, then the group needs to respect that there will be differences of opinions and learn to value diversity and multiple ways of interpreting events.

If teachers are going to reflect on their own professional practice, and that of others in their action learning team, there may be times when difficulties arise. Teaching has often been a solitary practice once the classroom door has been closed, which means that sharing practice and reflecting on it in a group can be a new phenomenon and challenging for teachers. It is especially difficult since the context in which team members are working is embedded in a particular historical, cultural and political environment. Despite these issues, ethical action learning will seek to ensure that all team members genuinely collaborate throughout all stages of the process.

The work of Bishop and Glynn (1999), although particularly dealing with their research in indigenous contexts, suggests that there need to be explicit group discussion and negotiation about the amount of collaboration expected from each participant. For example, a time limit may need to be set in terms of discussing a particular issue or the presentation of a case or story by one person. It may be the role of the group facilitator to help manage group discussions to ensure that an action learning meeting does not get bogged down discussing one issue or only focus on one person's needs, without real progress. This will help remove resentment later, because teachers are always time poor and the process must be seen to be worth the time and commitment they are investing. If there is an external partner involved as a team member, they must also be involved in any discussion about time limits. Questions of intellectual property must also be involved, as discussed in Chapter 6. Written reports and articles with shared authorship are important. Where one team member takes responsibility for authoring, other team members must have opportunities to see and comment on drafts.

Transparency

Transparent processes must be evident in both the enactment of action learning and in how these processes are accounted for in the school and wider community. Otherwise, the processes can be seen as closed and inaccessible to those who are not part of the action learning team. In our experience, where the composition of the team or the decisions about the issue are not clear, other members of the school community can feel left out. Sachs (2003) raises a number of valuable questions that are relevant to any discussion of transparency:

- Whose questions need to be on the agenda?
- Whose evidence?
- How is it to be gathered?
- How will it be used?

In addition, *how* decisions will be made and *who* will make them need to be clearly communicated.

Once it has been established that it is appropriate to gather evidence from students, other teachers or parents relevant to the questions being asked, then it is important to obtain their informed, and preferably written, consent.

Informed consent means the participants are aware of how the information they are contributing is to be used and of any risks involved. For example, it would be unethical for teachers to interview school students to ascertain their opinion about other teachers and then to make those students' individual opinions known to the teachers concerned. This would potentially expose the students to retribution because they have been so 'honest'. However, there may be ways of keeping students' identity confidential, by providing written transcripts of student opinions or combining the comments of a wide variety of students. This highlights the importance of ensuring ethical protocols are followed, particularly when stakeholders are invited to provide evidence. All stakeholders contributing to evidence gathering should, if at all possible, have a chance to read and verify their contribution. If there are dissenting opinions, these must be made explicit.

It is also ethical to acknowledge contributors in any report produced from the action learning process. Collaborative development towards any report or outcomes is also a way of ensuring 'fidelity to the stories that matter' (Groundwater-Smith and Mockler, 2007: 202). However, at some point, if a publicly available report about an action learning project is mandated, schools and teachers will need to decide whether they wish to use pseudonyms or whether they would prefer to publish their names. Participants have the right to be identified if they wish, just as they have the right to remain anonymous. Walford (2005) also points out that sometimes the promise of complete anonymity can be impossible, because a person can only be guaranteed anonymity if no one, including the researchers, knows the identity of the data source. If pseudonyms are to be used within a school context where most teachers know each other, it should be made explicit that, while attempts will be made to maintain confidentiality, this cannot always be guaranteed. For example, if a sensitive report is circulated to a small group of people, even using pseudonyms means that people may be identified just from the detail of the events described. This may become more of an issue if a school has public funding. In such cases, those involved in a particular project can be expected to publish reports, which may subsequently be used in further research and/or published on the Internet.

Ethical action

Action learning involves people taking actions that often have an impact on others. In schools, for example, the actions that a team decides to take will influence the experiences of students and other teachers in the school. It is therefore important to ensure that actions are ethical, with the team being confident that the action is well informed and clearly communicated. The degree of confidence necessary to recommend a proposed action depends somewhat on the potential consequences.

If, for example, a team seeking to enhance the sustainability of the school recommends that the hot-water temperature in taps be lowered by adjusting the heater thermostats, the likelihood of harm or disadvantage to others arising from this action is small. Hence, the degree of confidence in the evidence to support the action is also small. So too is there little need to quickly follow up to determine whether the action brought about the outcome that was sought. By contrast, a team seeking ways to improve classroom management in early high school years might recommend the introduction of graded classes based on student achievement on test scores. Such action has considerable potential to do harm. Therefore, the team would need to have a greater level of confidence for this action and should mount a sound argument after wide consultation. The basis for the recommendation should be subjected to extensive scrutiny. Furthermore, because of the potential harm, there is a need to immediately monitor the effects and for the team to be responsive to this feedback.

Goodwill is a precious thing, but ethical action demands more than good intentions. It requires careful assessment of the potential risks. It requires the degree of confidence in any decision to be matched with the potential consequences of the action. It also requires that the monitoring and review process be in line with the potential harm of these actions.

Accountability

Teachers are accountable to their many stakeholders. After a particular action learning process or project has concluded, it will be important to decide what has been achieved in light of the original goals, expectations and questions, particularly if public funding has been provided. Do the outcomes necessitate further exploration or is there a call to deliberate action to address particular difficulties identified? Sometimes the answers may be challenging to determine. If 'unwelcome truths' (Kemmis, 2006: 474) need to be shared with others, the action learning team must consider the effects of reporting these. Who should be the audience for these conversations? Team members must acknowledge that, in some cases, some of the findings may need to be withheld, if, for example, the participants would be easily identified and if the information may cause harm to the community's perception of them. Further, there are times when this decision may affect the transformative potential of the research, and team members must carefully weigh up the best course of action under such circumstances. At the same time, Hartog (2004: 400) reminds us that critical reflection on actions may require us to have courage to stand by our convictions. In a similar vein, Groundwater-Smith (2007: 10) suggests that there are times when we need

> to learn from each other and to break from the boundaries and constraints of habitual practice but the challenges are great. Learning to be defiant

against the odds of being compliant means learning how to challenge established social and political assumptions and develop resilience (Newman, 2006).

Conclusion

Building on Groundwater-Smith and Mockler (2007), it seems important that action learning processes need to incorporate trust and collaboration, as well as transparent ethical actions for which the team is accountable, if they are to be ethical. Although referring to the action research process, Zeichner's (2003) words provide a fitting conclusion to this discussion about ethical practice in action learning:

> The reality . . . is that the political and the critical are right there in front of us in our classrooms and other work sites and the choices we make everyday in our own work settings reveal our moral commitments with regard to social continuity and change whether we want to acknowledge it or not. We cannot be neutral.
>
> (Zeichner, 2003: 201)

Ethical action learning processes have the potential to enhance teachers' awareness of issues in their own practice. We believe that getting the ethics right in action learning processes will contribute to the eventual sustainability of teacher professional learning. The following chapter examines the issue of sustainability in more depth.

Chapter 9

Sustaining professional learning through action learning

> Sustainability by our definition requires continuous improvement, adaptation and collective problem solving in the face of complex challenges that keep arising.
>
> (Davies, 2006: 13)

Many school reforms are short-lived and often depend heavily on the enthusiasm of the original initiators/facilitators for ongoing success. If developed effectively, action learning processes can enhance the likelihood of sustained professional learning in schools and, hence, improve student learning outcomes over time. At the same time, they can provide opportunities for the development of leadership skills and the building of leadership capacity within schools. Given the accelerating rate of change required in society and thus in schools, the processes of action learning can be embedded in school cultures to provide tools to consider issues arising from this constant pressure to move forward.

This chapter draws on the preceding chapters to propose a model for sustainable professional learning in schools using action learning processes. It uses a case study to illustrate the model that was developed following an evaluative enquiry into the use of action learning as a professional learning tool in a large-scale, system-wide action learning project (Ewing *et al.*, 2004, 2005; Zeichner, 2003). Through this discussion we demonstrate that sustainability is not an endpoint but an ongoing process.

The case chosen for discussion has sustained action learning processes for over fifteen years. At different points during this timeframe, it has been carefully scrutinised to identify factors that are critical for sustaining professional learning (Ewing, 2002, 2006, 2008). From this, it is clear that a broad and collaborative school professional learning community, intelligent distributed leadership and programmed time for dedicated planning, discussion and reflection are all critical factors in enabling such sustainability. Further, these enabling factors need to come together in a synergy for sustainability to be optimised. This synergy is visually represented in the model following (Figure 9.1); however, it is acknowledged that any model

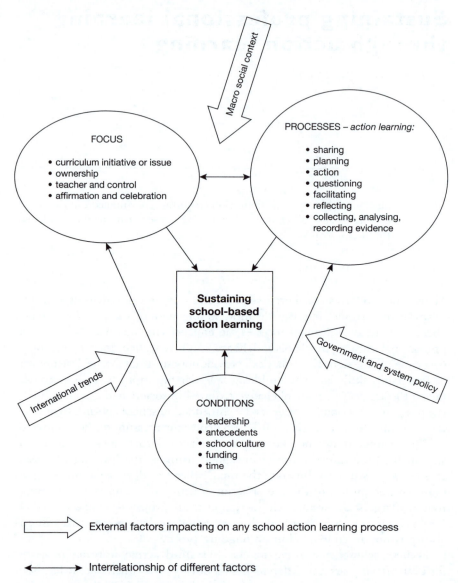

Figure 9.1 Factors identified as important in sustaining professional learning through action learning

(Adapted from Ewing *et al.*, 2005)

Explanatory note: *External factors* have been considered in some detail in earlier chapters. All schools are strongly influenced by the micro and macro socio-political context in which they are located (Grimmett and Fraser, 2008). International trends, governments and system policy are all part of this larger picture.

is a limited and often primitive representation of a dynamic and very fluid situation. This chapter discusses each element of the model more specifically and then raises several challenges to the sustainability of school reform, before considering the case study itself in more detail.

Conditions for sustainability

Leadership

The leaders of a school professional learning community must be actively committed to the learning of all its members, regardless of where an individual is up to on their own professional learning journey. We have discussed this at length in Chapter 3: 'Enabling action learning'. Resources therefore need to be allocated to support such learning within a shared collective and enable a focused vision that places student and teacher learning at the centre of the school's core business. The school executive needs to be actively supportive of any action learning set, whether or not executive members are part of the action learning team and regardless of whether it is a large- or small-scale project. At the same time, they must be aware that over-managing an action learning process may be intrusive. Ownership of, and responsibility for, the action learning activities should therefore be delegated to team members. In addition, the team coordinator(s) need to be strong but sensitive in their management of the group, able to maintain effective communication and give clear direction to all members of the team and other staff in the school (Ewing *et al.*, 2004).

Active and supportive leadership by the principal of a school is also central to the sustainability of the action learning process. The principal and school executive need to see the link between teacher learning and day-to-day classroom practice. Rather than seeing it as an optional 'extra', they need to find ways to embed collaborative teacher learning on site within the school planning initiatives and documents. In some cases, this leadership may be direct and directive, with the principal or deputy principal taking a 'hands-on' role, but in others, the senior executive takes a step back. In the most successful action learning processes, the team leaders are supported, and school leaders are able to provide the right amount of pressure where and when appropriate.

Antecedents

Schools and teachers who have been involved with successful change initiatives in the past are naturally more receptive to a new action learning enquiry (Fullan and Stiegelbauer, 1991; Smith and Lovat, 2003). As a result of such successful experiences, the broader school community is also likely to be more accepting of the necessity for change in the school.

School culture

Often, as has been discussed in the chapter on 'Positioning action learning', past professional learning in Australia and other western countries has been dictated by employers or education systems. This practice has often deskilled teachers (e.g. Day and Roberts-Holmes, 1998; Ramsey, 2000). Instead, a school culture that regards teachers as professionals who are actively responsible for their own learning, identifying relevant goals and establishing strategies to achieve these goals with other colleagues, has been shown to be much more successful in bringing about change (Elliott, 1991; Zeichner, 2003). Thus the workplace, as Revans (1983a) outlined, becomes a centre for conversations about learning and enquiry. There is a growing realisation that this kind of professional learning for teachers is critical for improving student learning outcomes (e.g. Cochran-Smith and Lytle, 1998; Darling-Hammond, 2000). Learning by teachers needs to be affirmed as part of their everyday working life, rather than something that is additional to their day-to-day practices. 'Sustainability is a conversation' (Smith *et al.*, 2007: 16), and a school culture in which both formal and informal conversations about learning, the future, our visions, expectations and assumptions take place is one where action learning processes are likely to be successful.

In addition, teachers need opportunities to have this kind of professional learning accredited. In recent years, this has been possible through the recording of, and reflection about, this kind of learning in professional learning portfolios, assessed by academics as part of an accreditation towards a postgraduate degree (Groundwater-Smith, 1999b; Ponte and Smit, 2008). Teachers need to be in control of their own professional learning, if change in schools is to be sustained beyond the length of a particular process, after specific project funding has ceased. From the outset, it is important for teachers to see themselves as authentic sources and creators of knowledge. They need to respect the knowledge that has become so much a part of who they are, which they often do not make explicit. Teachers who respect and understand themselves as learners and researchers feel empowered to generate new knowledge and understandings. Teachers also realise that teaching is a learning profession, and that each teacher has a professional responsibility to continue their own professional learning and that of their colleagues. The school culture therefore needs to generate a safe place where teachers feel respected, supported, powerful and intellectually challenged and where relationships allow high levels of trust and risk-taking. Students and parents need to feel similarly in their school and classrooms. They need to be respected as active participants in the change process.

In many schools where action learning processes have been sustained over a number of years, elements of professional learning communities (Ewing, 2002; Hargreaves, 2003; Hoban, 2002) were a long-standing part of the school culture. Professional learning had become integral to the strategic plans, policies and structures of these schools. This can be more challenging in large high schools, where learning community elements are sometimes characteristic of some faculties rather than the whole teaching staff (Ewing *et al.*, 2004). Where cross-faculty project teams are established, however, a richness of understanding across disciplines is likely to develop.

Funding and time

Funding must be found to provide substantial time to release teachers from normal classroom teaching, to establish systematic planning, discussion, observation and reflection sessions. To undertake systematic enquiry and professional learning, teachers need opportunities for thinking space to identify issues and set achievable goals; plan and discuss strategies; and review, critique and reflect on their practices. For this to happen, school leaders need to find organisational strategies that are built around the development of relationships and quality learning, rather than allow their schools to be 'ruled by the bell'. Further, after external funding is exhausted, school leaders must find ways to use school-allocated resources creatively to enable these professional learning processes to continue.

Action learning processes

There are also a number of factors derived from the action learning process itself that enable professional learning to be sustained. From the outset, although it seems obvious, it is important that all team members in the action learning set must develop a sound knowledge and understanding of the nature, implementation skills, processes and stages in action learning.

Other key factors enabling action learning to be sustained include sharing, planning, action, questioning, reflecting, observing and facilitating further action. They have been discussed at length in earlier chapters (see, particularly, Chapters 2, 3 and 6). A number of significant factors are highlighted below:

Leadership

Leadership within action learning teams has already been mentioned as a vital factor in sustaining action learning. Leadership responsibilities include:

- undertaking administrative arrangements related to organising time, locations and agendas for various meetings;
- facilitating essential communication between team members and between the team and other members of the executive and staff in a school or cluster of schools;
- negotiating with external project officers and academic partners, where relevant;
- ensuring that the team remains clearly directed and focused on its work;

- maintaining a positive emotional climate within the team and building cohesion, but, at the same time, allowing for individual viewpoints and constructive critique.

Sharing

Often, action learning teams explicitly state that they feel commitment to not only share their experiences with other teachers, but to use their under-standings and skills to provide opportunities for other staff to gain knowledge of, and develop, skills in action learning. The opportunity to share the action learning experience and the project with others through presentations and publications can itself encourage sustainability. Schools and school systems must find ways to share more widely the stories of the action learning journeys and to celebrate the findings and outcomes beyond their own school communities. As a profession, it is imperative that we find ways to communicate and celebrate success in school reform more broadly. Websites may be one way that this can happen more quickly, but sharing conferences are also important.

Integrating parents and community members into an extended action learning process through sharing can also be important in ensuring sustainability. Parents can be provided with information regarding the process itself, as well as its particular focus, how this is being developed and how it will benefit their children. They thus can become not only partners with their children in their learning, but also strong advocates of providing professional learning opportunities for teachers in the school.

Planning

The planning of an action learning process needs to ensure the projected outcomes are achievable. Parameters therefore must be carefully and collaboratively designed by the team. They then need to be refined within the specific context of a school workplace and its activities, so that they focus around outcomes that reflect priorities clearly identified by the school and the professional needs of teachers' everyday classroom practice. At the same time, plans must be realistic. In our view, plans that are too ambitious can falter because of their magnitude.

Facilitation

Ongoing effective relationships with external academic partners as critical friends (see Chapter 6, 'Facilitating action learning: The academic partner's role') can also be an important factor for some teams to sustain action learning in their school. For external 'experts' based in systems or universities to be useful, they must work *with* teachers in school contexts, recognising and affirming the teachers' knowledge and helping them to build new ideas and possibilities from research and learning processes. In addition, external partners need to be active participants in the school learning teams. Such a partnership requires some radical rethinking about traditional relationships and demands different expectations, roles and qualities of those working as critical friends with teacher action learning teams. As discussed earlier, thought must also be given to how an academic partner might withdraw from the project at an appropriate time.

Reflecting

Designated time and opportunity to evaluate and reflect allow teams, and thus schools, to review the goals, focus, organisation and effectiveness of their action learning processes. It also allows them to plan future action learning strategies as part of their whole-school development/strategic plan. Questioning at each stage of the action learning process will also be important for reflection. These questions will include those for the whole team (e.g. how are we progressing at this stage of the process?) and those for individual team members (e.g. what issues are surfacing for me?).

Collecting, analysing and recording evidence

Collecting, analysing and recording the evidence of learning and change must be planned from the outset to demonstrate and document ongoing and sustained teacher learning. Recording teacher and team learning is difficult to do retrospectively. Gathering evidence using a range of different tools is important. Developing analytical skills to analyse the evidence collected is crucial if schools are to provide evidence for sustained reform. Academic partners may be able to provide assistance to other team members by sharing their research analysis skills.

Ownership and control

The professional learning content may centre around a school need or system priority, or it may originate within a school or a cluster of schools in a particular area. The action learning team may also work with individual concerns of their members. Some examples include:

- improving student learning outcomes in a particular subject or discipline area;
- application of a particular pedagogical framework to improve teaching;
- developing more effective strategies to meet individual learner needs;
- working with a particularly challenging group of students.

Teachers need to be able to see that the focus of any action learning project directly relates to the core business of their classrooms and the school and they must have a sense of ownership and control of the process. The importance of a reform project directly relating to a school curriculum initiative must therefore be emphasised.

In addition, the sharing process discussed above may lead to celebratory activities and affirmation of their efforts.

Challenges to sustaining action learning

A number of factors can challenge and restrict the level of sustainability of action learning processes. In our experiences, two factors in particular have recurred in interviews and focus group discussions with teachers. These are outlined below.

First, the intensification of teachers' working lives continues to escalate. Action learning teams frequently refer to the increasing demands on their work as teachers. This issue underlines the importance of providing release time from normal teaching duties for teachers, if professional learning and development effectiveness is to be optimised and teacher burnout is to be avoided. This in turn has implications for funding for teacher release. At the same time, however, availability of sufficient appropriately qualified relief teachers can be an issue for schools, particularly in isolated or disadvantaged locations.

Second, negative attitudes of other staff who are not part of the action learning team can be a challenge, even if those staff members have chosen not to participate. This issue may be a result of these teachers' earlier less successful involvement in a change process. It can sometimes arise because teachers who are not initially part of a project team feel they have been left out. This difficulty highlights the importance of effective communication across the whole school and the need for the team leader to manage any potential emerging conflicts due to misunderstandings or misperceptions. In larger schools in particular, effective communication can be more challenging and therefore needs to be carefully addressed.

Case study: North Curl Curl Elementary School

The following case study describes ongoing sustained professional learning using action learning in one elementary school, located in suburban Sydney, over the past fifteen years. Students attending the school come from a diverse range of socio-economic contexts, and about 25 per cent have language backgrounds other than English. The staff profile currently includes several early career and temporary teachers, but the majority of teachers have more than ten years' experience. Parents are heavily involved in the school community. The school's enrolment has increased from around four hundred in 1994 to nearly seven hundred in 2008. The enabling factors described above have been used as a framework to organise the following case study discussion.

Workplace conditions

Leadership

The first action learning project began in 1994, with the then principal and her original action learning team, which included two assistant principals and two classroom teachers. Nias' (1995) evaluation of the school described the principal as a key factor in the school's approach to developing a professional learning community in which all stakeholders were valued. The principal was characterised as an open communicator who saw the professional learning journey of each staff member as unique and important. While her beliefs and actions were central to the success of the professional learning projects, her willingness to share the responsibility and decision-making with others keen to be involved proved even more valuable. She recognised potential and nurtured the capacities of others, encouraging them to participate in the leadership of the initial project, as well as subsequent projects.

The school executive was similarly supportive of classroom teachers who expressed a desire to be involved in the process and the projects. When an external academic partner was invited to join the project in 1995, the two assistant principals and several classroom teachers were keen to involve the partner in their classrooms to work alongside them as a critical friend.

Antecedents

The school's history, including, for example, its role in the NSW Department of Education's Reading Recovery initiative, indicates a history of ongoing commitment to improving student outcomes through teacher professional learning. The initial change project was funded by the Australian Government through a National Innovative Links grant in 1995. The school's overall aim was to improve student literacy outcomes and engagement using drama strategies and quality literary texts, particularly for students in years 3 and 4. While the specific focus has changed over time, the overall aim of improving student literacy outcomes remained constant until 2007, when a new Australian Government Quality Teaching Project focusing on mathematics commenced.

Each action learning project has built on earlier ones. For example, the initial project that focused on stage two literacy outcomes broadened to a whole-school project in 1996. Over time, those teachers who worked with the academic partner in turn mentored other colleagues, and staff development days provided opportunities for whole-school sharing. Each project has had a particular focus under the umbrella of the improvement of literacy outcomes. Particular projects have included:

- improvement in student narrative writing;
- improvement of students' understanding of transition from primary to high school;
- improved substantive communication outcomes; and
- teaching imaginatively to enhance students' creativity.

School culture: Elements of a professional learning community

Schools that can be characterised as 'professional learning communities/ cultures', 'communities of practice' or 'learning organisations' are more likely to be able to sustain initiatives. In brief, many of the features evident at Curl Curl North resonate with the factors elaborated earlier in the chapter. They include: effective communication; strong distributive leadership practices; collaborative relationships; enthusiasm; and a shared vision.

Funding

Over the years, funding for the different action learning projects has been provided through successful grant applications, including Innovative Links (1994–96); National Schools Network (1997–98, 2002); Innovative and Best Practice Project (1998–2000); a National Literacy Award (2001); University of Sydney Teaching Improvement Small Grant Partnerships (2001–03); Australian Government Quality Teaching Programme (2006–07); and Australian Literacy Educators Association (2008). These external funds have also been supplemented with school professional learning funding. The most important thing the funding enabled was release time for the teachers to meet for planning and reflection, both individually, with the academic partner, and as a group.

Action learning processes

With each new action learning team, knowledge and understanding of the nature and processes involved in action learning were critical and needed to be revisited. At the beginning of each of the action learning projects, individual teachers were released from the classroom to work with the academic partner in a whole group, and then individually, to identify their concerns or needs in light of system and school expectations. Strategic goals and directions were set, and relevant units of work and pedagogical strategies were discussed. Initially, each week over one or two terms, the academic partner modelled strategies in the classroom. The class teacher then built on these sessions in light of the class needs and her own focus for the particular unit of work. Over the years, the academic partner spent less time in the classrooms and more time in discussions with the action learning team.

Leadership within the team

One of the important features of the action learning projects at Curl Curl North was that they were teacher driven. While the principal always took an active role, ongoing leadership of each project was delegated to either a member of the executive or another teacher specifically interested in the particular project's focus.

Planning

Release time for planning was always cited by successive teams as vital to the success of the action learning process. The funding cited above enabled the school to build this release time into the school day.

Academic partner

As already mentioned, in 1995, the then principal engaged an academic partner to work with the teachers of stage two to enable them to understand and implement the new K-6 English syllabus (1994) and, through team teaching with the classroom teachers, to model strategies that would improve student engagement in literacy. The teachers subsequently controlled the whole process and identified their own professional needs and concerns in the context of their own classes. By 2008, the academic partner was acting as a facilitator for the whole-group discussion of the eight-member team involved in the Teaching Imaginatively Project. She regarded herself as superfluous. In July 2008, four of the team members presented at the Australian Literacy Education Association National Literacy Conference. The academic partner defines the process of working with the school as a positive synergy and terms it 'co-mentoring'. Her work in the classroom alongside the teachers interested in curriculum change and as a part of the action learning team has helped to keep her abreast of the pressures facing teachers and students. She has been able to use this in her work with pre-service teachers (Ewing, 2002, 2006).

Collecting, analysing and recording evidence

Action learning at Curl Curl North has included a range of data collection methods to evaluate the processes that have been employed, as well as the different projects over time, together with the impact on students' learning outcomes. These methods have included analysing students' results in New South Wales Basic Skills Tests in literacy and numeracy, as well as in Primary

Writing Assessment tasks. More recently, the new National Assessment programme has been examined. Examples of students' work have been collected and benchmarked, with permission from both students and parents. Between 1996 and 1999, for example, students' responses to test items requiring problem solving improved each year (Ewing, 2002). Similarly, children chosen for long-term profiling as they progressed from year 3 to year 5 demonstrated (2005–07) significant improvement (Ewing, 2008).

Evaluation and reflection

Teachers and students have reflected at several points during, and at the conclusion of, each project. Each teacher involved has been engaged in conversational interviews about the process, both with the academic partner and more formally with the principal of the school. Independent evaluators were also employed on two occasions (in 1998 and 2005) to conduct interviews with the teachers. A number of focus group discussions with groups of students have also been undertaken. One evaluator (Loughland, 2005: 7) writes:

> High expectations of the students were also apparent in the Year 4 classroom where the teacher was mentoring an early career teacher in literacy pedagogy. The students were able to describe to me how the activities led them to a deep understanding of the themes of two texts, Boy Overboard and The Burnt Stick . . . The conversation I had with these four students revealed their deep understanding of characters, themes and meaning of texts.

This finding was supported by the teachers, who noticed that the students engaged with texts at a deeper level after drama activities and strategies were introduced at the beginning of the year. A selection of student reflections about the use of drama in their learning about the stolen generation is provided below:

- 'Drama was good because we got to feel how John Jagamarra felt.'
- 'I think it was a great way of learning what happened with Aboriginals and why it happened.'
- 'I liked writing what it was like at Pearl Bay Mission that put your mind to the text and you had to think what is was like back then.'

(Ewing, 2006)

In each project there has been a body of evidence confirming that the students' understanding of complex issues from a range of different perspectives has informed their growth in critical literacy. Each of the teachers reflected that their students' oracy, reading and writing skills had improved markedly over the project. The principal, school executive, teachers and students feel strongly that the use of drama with authentic texts has been an important factor in the improvement of school literacy outcomes over time and in the growth in the school as a professional learning community. In addition, teachers commented on the improvement in students' overall ability to work cooperatively. Many of these outcomes and the understandings the students developed cannot be easily measured in the kinds of test situation that currently dominate our assessment practices. Yet this kind of more qualitative evidence is also important.

Challenges

It would be wrong to suggest that these projects have been easy. Time to continue with the action learning projects given increasing system demands and staff turnover have been the two constant challenges at the school and are expressed in the evaluations of particular projects. At the beginning of each school year, it has been critical to stop and reflect on the particular action learning project being undertaken and ensure that new staff understand the principles and have an opportunity to be involved where appropriate.

Conclusions and recommendations

There are several issues that emerge from the experience of investigating the sustainability of professional learning through action learning processes. One of the most frequently cited results of participation in sustained action learning projects and ongoing professional learning is the level of collegiality that forms within action learning teams and, in some cases, across entire schools.

In addition, over the long term, a return of excitement and enthusiasm about teaching seems to be generated through the action learning process, perhaps because teachers' work is being validated. Teachers also report more confidence about their abilities to promote student learning, along with a greater conviction about the importance of student voice (Groundwater-Smith and Mockler, 2003) in the teaching and learning process. Hargreaves (2003) recently reported Canadian research that demonstrated that, after a change project had ended, the level of collegiality attained during the project lessened because there was no longer an explicit motivation to support its continuance. Both formal and informal professional learning conversations thus need to be embedded within school strategic plans.

To return to the opening quote by Davies (2006), it is clear from the case study that learning processes, when effectively understood and implemented, can facilitate continuous improvement and adaptation in ever-changing and increasingly challenging school contexts. To date, however, there is little long-term documentation of successful, sustained school reform over more than five years. It is our view that large-scale longitudinal analysis is needed to examine how schools with such enabling conditions continue to renew and reinvigorate, despite changes in executive and teaching staff. Curl Curl North is an example of a school that has sustained its change process for over fifteen years through the use of action learning.

Chapter 10

Epilogue: extending action learning

> Learning is at the core of rethinking teacher professionalism. As an individual and collective goal, teachers should be seen to practice the value of learning, both with their colleagues and with their students. By recasting themselves as learners, the social relations of schools and the relations between teachers and teachers, teachers and students, and teachers and their communities, will be fundamentally reshaped. Learning rather than teaching becomes the core activity of teacher and student life in schools.
>
> (Sachs, 2003: 31)

There is one statement that all teachers agree upon – as we progress into the twenty-first century, teaching is becoming more complex. Not only is teaching influenced by changing curriculum, the types of student, resources, assessment, existing approaches, as well as school and government policies, knowledge is growing exponentially, and information and communication technologies are permeating every aspect of education. Because teaching is becoming increasingly complex, changing practice is not a simple process, hence the need for a sophisticated framework to initiate and sustain teacher learning. This book has argued for the usefulness of action learning as one such framework. This is because a key feature of action learning is that it is underpinned by multiple processes and conditions to support teacher learning. Action learning encourages teachers not only to reflect and share ideas among a small group, but also to seek feedback from colleagues and students while experimenting with their practice. As shown in Figure 9.1, the interaction of the action learning processes is enhanced by the presence of certain conditions such as time, antecedents, funding, school culture, leadership and collegiality in a school.

The question remains, why should teachers engage in professional learning, which is time consuming and can be confronting to their beliefs and practices? According to Sachs (2003), learning by teachers is at the heart of being a professional. Engaging in action learning gives teachers responsibility to make judgements that shape their identity and supports them in developing a learning culture within a school. The seven principles that shape the teacher identity of being a 'postmodern professional', as described by Hargreaves and Goodson (1996), are promoted by action learning:

- increased opportunity and responsibility to exercise *discretionary judgement* over the issues of teaching, curriculum and care that affect one's students;
- opportunities and expectations to engage with the *moral and social purposes* and value of what teachers teach, along with major curriculum and assessment matters in which these purposes are embedded;
- commitment to working with colleagues in *collaborative cultures* of help and support as a way of using shared expertise to solve the ongoing problems of professional practice, rather than engaging in joint work as a motivational device to implement the external mandate of others;
- occupational *heteronomy* rather than self-protective *autonomy,* where teachers work authoritatively yet openly and collaboratively with other partners in the wider community (especially parents and students themselves), who have a significant stake in the students' learning;
- a commitment to active *care* and not just anodyne *service* for students. Professionalism must in this sense acknowledge and embrace the emotional as well as the cognitive dimensions of teaching, and also recognise the skills and dispositions that are essential to committed and effective caring;
- a self-directed search and struggle for *continuous learning* related to one's expertise and standards of practice, rather than compliance with the enervating obligations of *endless change* demanded by others (often under the guise of continuous learning or improvement);
- the creation and recognition of high task *complexity,* with levels of status and reward appropriate to such complexity.
  (Hargreaves and Goodson, 1996: 20–21, emphasis in original)

More than ever, teachers need to reflect and discuss with each other about why they teach the way they do and be encouraged collaboratively to 'think outside of the square they teach in'. When this is the case, teachers become knowledge producers about their own classrooms and are engaged in studying their own practice as professionals.

Of the frameworks for teacher learning identified in Chapter 2, we believe that it is action learning that encourages teachers to be professionals and is the most likely to lead to change in classroom teaching practices. Because 'change is a process, not an event', changes in teaching practice do not happen instantaneously, and so efforts for change need to be accompanied by processes and conditions to support teacher learning. As argued in Chapter 4 and developed in Chapter 9, it is not one learning process or one condition of learning that leads to change in teaching, but a combination that enhances itself as a synergy.

Final thoughts

There are some interesting, and possibly unexpected, outcomes for teachers when they participate in action learning. One of the most powerful is that they may develop a better understanding of how they learn professionally. By monitoring their own learning, teachers can become aware of the processes and conditions that 'work for them', so that they become metacognitive about their own learning (Hoban *et al.*, 2005). Teachers can then begin to manage their own professional learning and take opportunities when they arise to utilise different forms of teacher learning. It means that teachers can plan their own professional learning over a long period of time, such as a year, using existing opportunities, including one-off workshops or professional development days. The important point is that teachers will get more value out of these one-shot events because they are happening in context with their own long-term professional learning goals that teachers are designing and self-managing.

One form of professional learning may also evolve into another. For example, teachers who participate in action learning for several months may decide on a question that they would like answered about student learning. It may eventuate that the best way for the question to be answered is by gathering evidence using surveys, individual interviews or focus groups, as highlighted in Chapter 7. In this scenario, teachers can participate in action research and systematically gather evidence to address a specific research question, which can then be shared or critiqued by the group or set.

A third outcome is that action learning, which usually only involves four to eight teachers, can be scaled up to involve a whole school or even a whole school district. For example, six teachers who were involved in action learning over a period of six months may split up and become the team leaders for other action learning sets or groups in the school. These processes can be further scaled up, with teachers in small groups in many schools interacting with facilitators who work across a whole school district (Borko, 2004).

One final consideration that teachers need to be aware of is that action learning can be intense, uncomfortable and time consuming. As highlighted in Chapter 8, sometimes action learning makes teachers feel vulnerable because they are exposed to the critique of others. For this reason, at the beginning of the action learning, time needs to be allocated for teachers to develop an understanding of the action learning processes and to deduce 'ground rules' for discussion, especially considering the ethics involved as explained in Chapter 8. It is also possible to engage in action learning in restricted timeframes. For example, one school that had a team engaging in action learning during terms 2 and 3 of a school year decided to stop in the last term of the year, owing to other time-consuming activities, such as reports, school prize-giving nights and plays. In the following year, the teachers resumed their action learning, which focused on a project that needed to be achieved over a school term. They held team meetings every two weeks to maintain the sharing of experiences and continually modified their action plans to achieve the team goal.

The best way for schools to manage change in the twenty-first century is to redesign themselves to become learning environments for their teachers. According to Sarason (1990), the quality of student learning in a school depends on the quality of teacher learning. Yet the organisation of many schools focuses almost exclusively on ways to enhance student learning, without consideration for structures to support teacher learning. When reorganising schools as learning environments for teachers, administrators need to think about the type of learning in which they wish teachers to engage. The commonly used one-off workshops and professional development days have their place, but action learning is a framework that enhances professionalism and can be a platform for a lifelong approach to teacher learning.

Glossary

Academic partner see *External partner*.

Action learning A framework for professional learning used to address problems or issues that arise in workplaces, originating in business management literature in the mid 1940s. In an educational context, essentially, action learning involves a small group of teachers regularly reflecting and sharing their experiences as a community, to help them understand or address an individual or shared issue, problem or project.

Action learning set A group of members from different parts and/or levels of an organisation established to work together in action learning.

Action learning team see *Action learning set*.

Action research A framework for professional learning that involves systematic enquiry and the gathering of information, originating in the social sciences in the 1940s. While its process has many similarities with action learning, it is distinguished by its emphasis on systematic data collection for research purposes that is made publicly available.

AGQTP Australian Government Quality Teaching Programme – An initiative established in 2000 to raise the quality, professionalism and status of Australian teachers and school leaders. The programme funds various projects at a national and state/territory level in a range of priority areas, including literacy, numeracy, science and technology, indigenous education, civics and values. See also *QTAL*.

Antecedents A preceding circumstance, cause or event, in this context, that facilitates action learning.

Collective reflection The social or organised sharing of events, ideas and theories to make sense of an organisational experience or problem.

Community of learners Particular kind of network or group of people who are engaging collaboratively in a learning process. See Lave and Wenger (1991) and Wenger (1998).

Community of practice A social system of knowledge production and exchange among a group that shares expertise in a particular field of practice, about which it interacts and seeks to improve the ways things are done.

Critical friend   The ideal role played by an external partner in the action learning process, providing both a trusted advisory function and objective review and analysis where necessary. See also *External partner*.

DET   New South Wales, Australia's Department of Education and Training – the state government agency that delivers public education and training for children during the compulsory years of schooling (kindergarten to year 10) and senior secondary education leading to the award of the NSW Higher School Certificate (years 11 to 12).

Discourse community   A concept whereby the people who use and help to create a particular field or way of thinking are linked together in a network or share a common identity.

Distributed leadership   A shared and collaborative approach to leadership of an organisation or school.

Elementary school   An institution where children receive the first stage of compulsory education, known as elementary or primary education. In Australia this is approximately between the ages of five and twelve. (Also referred to as primary school.)

External partner   A person outside the school, often a consultant or an academic from a university, who sponsors and facilitates the action learning process, providing advice where necessary. See also *Critical friend*.

Focus group   A form of qualitative research data collection where a collection of people are asked questions about their views on a particular topic or concept in an interactive group setting.

Learning community   see *Community of learners*

Pedagogy   The art and science of teaching. The term is normally used to refer to various types or styles of instruction used by teachers.

Peer observation   Observing of a colleague's classroom teaching, on equal terms. The aim, in an action learning context, is not to judge but to stimulate professional conversation and ideas.

Productive pedagogy   A framework for quality teaching developed in Queensland, based on the authentic pedagogy framework developed by Ron Newman and Associates at the University of Wisconsin in the 1990s.

Professional learning   A long-term approach, with teacher input into the content accompanied by a framework with multiple teacher learning processes and conditions to sustain learning in the school context.

Professional learning community   A group of professionals who trust each other and communicate honestly and often engage in professional conversations and learning opportunities to improve their knowledge and practices. See also *Community of practice*.

Project team   A group that is defined and limited by a particular task or project.

QTAL   Quality Teaching Action Learning – A NSW Department of Education and Training project, funded under the Australian Government Quality Teaching Programme (see *AGQTP*). The aim of the project was to investigate the dimensions of quality teaching using action learning.

Quality Teaching Framework   A teaching model released by the NSW Department of Education and Training in 2003, based on both Productive Pedagogy (Education Queensland) and Authentic Pedagogy (Newman and Associates). The model can be applied to all stages, across all key learning areas, and is based on three pedagogical dimensions: intellectual quality, quality learning environment and significance.

Reading Recovery   An initiative developed by renowned New Zealand educator Dame Marie Clay. The NSW government programme aims to offer children in year 1 of schooling, identified as experiencing some difficulty with learning to read, daily one-on-one sessions to help them develop confidence and improve their literacy skills.

Reflective records   The documentation of an account of an experience, event or process as a source of evidence in action learning. This can take the form of entirely open-ended, unfettered writing about almost anything related to the topic being addressed, or it can be guided by a scaffold of questions.

Release time   When a teacher is released from classroom teaching duties, either on a regular basis or for a specific purpose or project.

Stage   The level of achievement of particular groups of students, as determined by an educational syllabus. Also commonly a group of classes of similar age organised to learn the same syllabus content (e.g. elementary school years 5 and 6 typically are referred to as 'stage three').

Student work samples   Products or excerpts of work undertaken by students. These can be used to demonstrate progress and provide a source of evidence for how an innovation or strategy may be improving student learning outcomes.

Substantive communication   An element of the NSW Quality Teaching Framework.

References

Altrichter, H., Posch, P. and Somekh, B. (1993) *Teachers investigate their work: an introduction to the methods of action research*, London: Routledge.

Andrews, D. and Lewis, M. (2002) 'The experiences of a professional community: teachers developing a new image of themselves and their workplace', *Educational Research*, 44(3): 237–54.

Apple, M. (1990) *Ideology and curriculum*, 2nd edn, New York: Routledge.

Argyris, C. and Schön, D. A. (1974) *Theory in practice: increasing professional effectiveness*, San Francisco, CA: Jossey-Bass.

Ary, D., Cheser Jacobs, L., Razavieh, A. and Sorensen, C. (2006) *Introduction to research in education*, 7th edn, Belmont, CA: Thomson Wadsworth.

Aubusson, P. and Griffin, J. (2008) 'High support, high challenge, high learning: science-techno museum report', Sydney: UTS.

Aubusson, P., Brady, L. and Dinham, S. (2006) 'Action learning. What works?', Research report prepared for the New South Wales Department of Education and Training, Sydney: NSW DET.

Aubusson, P., Steele, F., Brady, L. and Dinham, S. (2007) 'Action learning in teacher learning community formation: information or transformative?', *Teacher Development*, 11: 133–48.

Aubusson, P., Buchanan, J., Schuck, S. and Russell, T. (2008) 'Making sense of teaching through shared observation and conversation', Paper presented at the Self-study of Teacher Education Practices Conference, Herstmonceux, East Sussex, England, 3–7 August.

Austen, J. (2008) *Pride and prejudice*, Adelaide: Bookwise International.

Baird, J. R. (1992) 'Collaborative reflection, systematic enquiry, better teaching', in T. Russell and H. Munby (eds) *Teachers and teaching: from classroom to reflection*, New York: Falmer Press.

Baird, J., Mitchell, I. and Northfield, J. (1987) 'Teachers as researchers: the rationale, the reality', *Research in Science Education*, 17: 129–38.

Barthes, R. (1982) *Barthes: selected writings*, London: Fontana Collins.

Bell, B. and Gilbert, J. (1994) 'Teacher development as professional, personal, and social development', *Teaching and Teacher Education*, 10(5): 483–97.

Bereiter, C. and Scardamalia, M. (1993) *Surpassing ourselves: an inquiry into the nature and implications of expertise*, Chicago, IL: Open Court.

Bierema, L. (1998) 'Fitting action learning to corporate programs', *Performance Improvement Quarterly*, 11(1): 86–107.

Biggs, J. (1993) 'From theory to practice: a cognitive systems approach', *Higher Education Research and Development*, 12(1): 73–85.

Bishop, R. and Glynn, T. (1999) *Culture counts*, Palmerston North: Dunmore Press.

Boddy, D. (1991) 'Supervisory development', in M. Pedler (ed.) *Action learning in practice*, Aldershot: Gower Publishing.

Borko, H. (2004) 'Professional development and teacher learning: mapping the terrain', *Educational Researcher*, 33(8): 3–15.

Bourner, T. and Frost, C. (1996) 'Experiencing action learning', *Employee Counselling Today*, 8(6): 11–18.

Burton, D. and Bartlett, S. (2005) *Practitioner research for teachers*, London: Paul Chapman.

Caldwell, B. and Spinks, J. (1998) *Beyond the self-managing school*, London: Falmer Press.

Campbell, E. (2003) *The ethical teacher*, Berkshire: Open University Press.

Clandinin, D. J. and Connelly, F. M. (1996) 'Teachers' professional knowledge landscapes – stories of teachers – school stories – stories of schools', *Educational Researcher*, 25(3): 24–30.

Cochran-Smith, M. and Lytle, S. (1998) 'Teacher research: the question that persists', *International Journal of Leadership in Education*, 1: 19–36.

Cooper, C. and Boyd, J. (1994) *Collaborative approaches to professional learning and reflection*, Launceston: Global Learning Communities.

Cox, E. (2003) 'Creating socially competent and ethical schools', *Independent Education*, 33: 16–19 (available online at http://search.informit.com.au.ezproxy2.library.usyd.edu.au/fullText;dn=130658;res=).

Craft, A. (2000) *Continuing professional development: a practical guide for teachers and schools*, London: RoutledgeFalmer.

Crowther, F., Kaagan, S., Ferguson, M. and Hann, L. (2002) *Developing teacher leaders*, Thousand Oaks, CA: Corwin.

Cusins, P. (1995) 'Action learning revisited', *Industrial and Commercial Training*, 27(4): 3–10.

Cusins, P. (1996) 'Action learning revisited', *Employee Counselling Today*, 8(6): 19–26.

Darling-Hammond, L. (ed.) (1994) *Professional development schools: schools for developing a profession*, New York: Teachers College Press.

Darling-Hammond, L. (1998) 'Teacher learning that supports student learning', *Educational Leadership*, 55(2): 6–11.

Darling-Hammond, L. (2000) 'Teacher quality and student achievement', *Education Policy Archives*, 8(1) (available online).

Davies, B. (2006) *Leading the strategically focused school*, London: Paul Chapman Publishing.

Day, C. (1999) *Developing teachers: the challenges of lifelong learning*, London: Falmer Press.

Day, C. and Roberts-Holmes, G. (1998) 'The best of times, the worst of times: stories of change and professional development in England', *Change*, 1(1): 15–31.

Dewey, J. (1916) *Democracy and education*, New York: Macmillan.

Dewey, J. (1933) *How we think: a restatement of the relation of reflective thinking to the educative process*, 2nd edn, Boston, MA: Heath and Co.

Dewey, J. (1938) *Experience and education*, New York: Collier Books.

Dewey, J. (1975) *Moral principles in education*, Carbondale, IL: Southern Illinois University Press.

Dinham, S. (2005) 'Principal leadership for outstanding educational outcomes', *Journal of Educational Administration*, 43(4): 338–56.

Dinham, S. (2007a) 'How schools get moving and keep improving: leadership for teacher learning, student success and school renewal', *Australian Journal of Education*, 51(3): 263–75.

Dinham, S. (2007b) 'The dynamics of creating and sustaining learning communities', *Unicorn*, Refereed article online, ORA43: 1–16.

Dinham, S. (2007c) *Leadership for exceptional educational outcomes*, Teneriffe: Post Pressed.

Dinham, S. (2008) 'Counting the numbers in educational change', *The Australian Educational Leader*, 30(1): 56–7.

Dinham, S., Aubusson, P. and Brady, L. (2008) 'Distributed leadership as a factor in and outcome of teacher action learning', *International Electronic Journal for Leadership in Learning*, 12(4): 1–17 (available online).

Dixon, N. (1998) 'Action learning: more than just a task force', *Performance Improvement Quarterly*, 11(1): 44–58.

Donnelly, K. (2007) *Dumbing down: outcomes-based and politically correct – the impact of the culture wars on our schools*, Prahran, Victoria: Hardie Grant Books.

DuFour, R. (2004) 'What is a professional learning community', *Educational Leadership*, 61(8): 6–11.

Elliott, J. (1991) *Action learning for educational change*. Philadelphia: Open University Press.

Erickson, G., Farr Darling, L. and Clarke, A. (2005) 'Constructing and sustaining communities of inquiry in teacher education', in G. Hoban (ed.) *The missing links of teacher education design: developing a multi-linked conceptual framework*, Dordrecht: Springer.

Ewing, R. (2002) 'Framing a professional learning community: an Australian case study', *Curriculum Perspectives*, 22(3): 23–32.

Ewing, R. (2006) 'Reading to allow spaces to play', in R. Ewing (ed.) *Beyond the reading wars. Towards a balanced approach to helping children learn to read*, Sydney: Primary English Teaching Association.

Ewing, R. (2008) 'Improving critical literacy pedagogy and outcomes through creative arts', Paper presented at Future Directions in Literacy Conference 'Local conversations', University of Sydney, 5–6 September.

Ewing, R., Smith, D., Anderson, M., Gibson, R. and Manuel, J. (2004) 'Teachers as learners', Australian Government quality teaching action learning for school teams project evaluation report, Division of Professional Learning, Faculty of Education & Social Work, University of Sydney (available online at http://qtp.nsw.edu.au/ResourceDocuments/Extract_Report.pdf).

Ewing, R. A., Hoban, G., Anderson, J., Herrington, T., Kervin, L. and Smith, D. L. (2005) *Evaluative inquiry into the sustainability of professional learning through school-based action learning*, Sydney: NSW DET.

Fendler, L. (2003) 'Teacher reflection in a hall of mirrors: historical influences and political reverberations', *Educational Researcher*, 32(3): 16–25.

Fogwill, S. and Aubusson, P. (2006) 'Student generated analogies in high school physics', Paper presented at the Australasian Science Education Research Association, University of Canberra, July.

Fullan, M. (1982) *The meaning of educational change*, Toronto: The Ontario Institute for Studies in Education.

Fullan, M. (1993) *Change forces: probing the depths of educational reform*, Bristol, PA: Falmer Press.

Fullan, M. (1999) *Change forces: the sequel*, London: Falmer Press.

Fullan, M. and Stiegelbauer, D. (1991) *The true meaning of educational change*, New York: Teachers College Press.

Ghaye, A. and Ghaye, K. (1998) *Teaching and learning through critical reflective practice*, London: David Fulton.

Giles, D. (1997) 'Teamworking at Williams Grand Prix engineering', in M. Pedler (ed.) *Action learning in practice*, 3rd edn, Aldershot, UK: Gower Publishing.

Gonczi, A. P. and Riordan, G. P. (2002) 'Measuring and reporting on discipline and student suspensions in NSW government schools', Report prepared for the NSW Minister for Education and Training, Mr John Watkins and Taskforce VAR, Sydney University of Technology.

Gregory, M. (1994) 'Accrediting work-based learning: action learning – a model for empowerment', *Journal of Management Development*, 13(4): 41–52.

Griffith, M. (2003) *Action for social justice in education: fairly different*, Philadelphia: Open University Press.

Grimmett, P. and Fraser, S. (2008) 'Legitimacy and identity in teacher education: a micro-political struggle constrained by (and sometimes superseded by) macro-political pressures', Keynote address at Australian Teacher Educators Annual Conference, Maroochidore, Queensland.

Gronn, P. (2002) 'Distributed leadership', in K. Leithwood and P. Hallinger (eds) *Second international handbook of educational leadership and administration*, Dordrecht: Kluwer.

Grossman, P. and Wineburg, S. (2000) *What makes the teacher community different from a gathering of teachers?*, Washington, DC: Center for the Study of Teaching and Policy, University of Washington.

Grossman, P., Wineburg, S. and Woolworth, S. (2001) 'Toward a theory of teacher community', *Teachers College Record*, 103(6): 942–1012.

Groundwater-Smith, S. (1999a) 'Participative learning: the school as a learning community and as a member of a National Reform Organisation', in J. Retallick (ed.) *Learning communities in education*, London: Routledge.

Groundwater-Smith, S. (1999b) 'Work matters: the professional learning portfolio', Paper presented at the PEPE Conference, Christchurch, New Zealand, January.

Groundwater-Smith, S. (2007) 'Practitioner researchers: today's children of Mother Courage. What can we learn from them?', Paper presented at the Communities and Change Research Festival, University of Sydney, October.

Groundwater-Smith, S. and Mockler, N. (2002) 'Building knowledge, building professionalism: the coalition of knowledge building schools and teacher professionalism', Paper presented at the Australian Association for Educational Research Annual Conference.

Groundwater-Smith, S. and Mockler, N. (2003) *Learning to listen: listening to learn*, Sydney: MLC School and the Centre for Practitioner Research, University of Sydney.

Groundwater-Smith, S. and Mockler, N. (2007) 'Ethics in practitioner research: an issue of quality', *Research Papers in Education*, 22(2): 199–211.

Hammersley, M. (2007) 'Educational research and teaching: a response to Hargreaves' TTA lecture', in M. Hammersley (ed.) *Educational research and evidence-based practice*, Milton Keynes: Open University Press.

Hargreaves, A. (1994) *Changing teachers, changing times: teachers' work and culture in the postmodern age*, London: Cassell.

Hargreaves, A. (2003) *Teaching in the knowledge society: education in the age of insecurity*, New York: Teachers College Press.

Hargreaves, A. (2007a) 'Teaching as a research-based profession', in M. Hammersley (ed.) *Educational research and evidence-based practice*, Milton Keynes: Open University Press.

Hargreaves, A. (2007b) 'In defence of research for evidence-based teaching: a rejoinder to Hammersley', in M. Hammersley (ed.) *Educational research and evidence-based practice*, Milton Keynes: Open University Press.

Hargreaves, A. and Goodson, I. (1996) 'Teachers' professional lives: aspirations and actualities', in I. Goodson and A. Hargreaves (eds) *Teachers' professional lives*, London: Falmer Press.

Hargreaves, D. H. (2000) 'The knowledge creating school', in B. Moon, J. Butcher and E. Bird (eds) *Leading professional development in education*, London: RoutledgeFalmer.

Hartog, M. (2004) 'Critical action learning: teaching business ethic', *Reflective Practice*, 5(3): 395–407 (available online).

Hatton, N. and Smith, D. (1994) 'Facilitating reflection: issues and research', Paper presented at the 24th Conference of the Australian Teacher Education Association, Brisbane, 3–6 July (ERIC Document Reproduction Service No ED375110).

Hatton, N. and Smith, D. (1995) 'Reflection in teacher education: towards definition and implementation', *Teaching and Teacher Education*, 11(1): 33–49.

Hill, G. (2002) *Critical friendship*, Australia: Mottram d'Hill & Associates.

Hoban, G. F. (1996) 'A professional development model based on interrelated principles of teacher learning', Unpublished doctoral dissertation, Vancouver, Canada: University of British Columbia.

Hoban, G. F. (2000a) 'Making practice problematic: listening to student interviews as a catalyst for teacher reflections', *Asia-Pacific Journal of Teacher Education*, 28(2): 133–47.

Hoban, G. F. (2000b) 'Using a reflective framework to study teaching-learning relationships', *Reflective Practice*, 1(2): 165–83.

Hoban, G. F. (2002) *Teacher learning for educational change: a systems thinking approach*, Buckingham and Philadelphia: Open University Press.

Hoban, G. F. (2004) 'Enhancing action learning with student feedback', *Action Learning: Research and Practice*, 1(2): 203–18.

Hoban, G. F. and Erickson, G. (2004) 'Dimensions of learning for long-term professional development: comparing approaches from education, business and medical contexts', *Journal of In-service Education*, 30(2): 301–23.

Hoban, G. F. and Hastings, G. (2006) 'Developing different forms of student feedback to promote teacher reflection: a ten year collaboration', *Teaching and Teacher Education*, 22: 1006–19.

Hoban, G. F., Butler, S. and Lesley, L. (2005) 'The dynamics of teacher learning in professional development: a collaborative self-study', *Studying Teacher Education*.

Hoban, G., Hastings, G., Luccarda, C. and Lloyd, D. (1997) 'Faculty based professional development as an action learning community', *Australian Science Teachers Journal*, 43(3): 49–54.

Hodkinson, P. and Hodkinson, H. (2003) 'Individuals, communities of practice and the policy context: school-teachers learning in their workplace', *Studies in Continuing Education*, 25(1): 3–21.

Hoyle, E. and John, P. (1995) *Professional knowledge and professional practice*, New York: Cassell.

Huberman, M. (1990) 'The model of an independent artist in teachers professional relations', in J. W. Little and M. W. McLaughlin (eds) *Teachers work*, New York: Teachers College Press.

Huberman, M. (1995) 'Networks that alter teaching', *Teachers and Teaching: Theory and Practice*, 1(2): 193–221.

Inglis, S. (1994) *Making the most of action learning*, Hampshire: Gower Publishing.

Johnson, N. (1999) 'Meeting the challenge: becoming learning communities', in J. Retallick, B. Cocklin and K. Coombe (eds) *Learning communities in education*, London: Routledge.

Kember, D. (2000) *Action learning and action research*, London: Kogan Page.

Kemmis, S. (2006) 'Participatory research and the public sphere', *Educational Action Research*, 14(4): 459–76.

Kemmis, S. (2007) 'Action research', in M. Hammersley (ed.) *Educational research and evidence-based practice*, Milton Keynes: Open University Press.

Kemmis, S. and McTaggart, R. (1988) *The action research planner*, Melbourne: Deakin University.

Kemmis, S. and McTaggart, R. (2005) 'Participatory action research, communicative action and the public sphere', in N. Denzin and Y. Lincoln (eds) *The Sage handbook of qualitative research*, 3rd edn, Thousand Oaks, CA: Sage.

Keys, L. (1996) 'Action learning: executives' development of choice for the 1990s', *Journal of Management Development*, 13(8): 50–6.

Kolb, D. A. (1984) *Experiential learning: experience as the source of learning*, Englewood Cliffs, NJ: Prentice Hall.

Koo, M. (2002) 'The missing critical friends' voices: an angel's heart or a beautiful mind', Paper presented at Australian Association for Research in Education Annual Conference, Brisbane.

Korthagen, F. A., Kessels, J., Koster, B., Lagerwerf, B. and Wubbels, T. (2001) *Linking practice and theory: the pedagogy of realistic teacher education*, Mahwah, NJ: Lawrence Erlbaum Associates.

Korthagen, F. A. and Vasalos, A. (2005) 'Levels in reflection: core reflection as a means to enhance professional growth', *Teachers and Teaching: Theory and Practice*, 11(1): 47–71.

LaBoskey, V. K. (1994) *Development of reflective practice*, New York: Teachers College Press.

Lanahan, E. and Maldonado, L. (1998) 'Accelerated decision-making via action learning at the federal Deposit Insurance Corporation', *Performance Improvement Quarterly*, 11(1): 74–85.

Lave, J. and Wenger, E. (1991) *Situated learning: legitimate peripheral participation*, Cambridge: Cambridge University Press.

Lewin, K. (1946) 'Action research and minority problems', *Journal of Social Issues*, (1): 34–46.

Lewis, A. (1991) 'An in-company program', in M. Pedler (ed.) *Action learning in practice*, Aldershot: Gower Publishing.

Lortie, D. C. (1975) *Schoolteacher: a sociological study*, Chicago: University of Chicago Press.

Loughland, A. (2005) 'Professional learning evaluation', Unpublished reports, Curl Curl North and Crown Street Primary Schools.

Loughran, J. J. (1995) 'Practicing what I preach: modelling reflective practice to student teachers', *Research in Science Education*, 25(4): 431–51.

Loughran, J. J. (1996) *Developing reflective practice: learning about teaching and learning through modelling*, London: Falmer Press.

Lyons, F. (2003) 'Customer-led learning environments: industry–university partnerships', Proceedings of HERDSA Conference, Christchurch, New Zealand.

McGill, I. and Beaty, L. (1995) *Action learning: a guide for professional, management and educational development*, London: Kogan Page.

McGill, I. and Beaty, L. (2001) *Action learning*, 2nd edn, London: Kogan Page.

McGill, I. and Brockbank, A. (2004) *The action learning handbook*, London: RoutledgeFalmer.

McLaughlin, M. (1997) 'Rebuilding teacher professionalism in the United States', in A. Hargreaves and R. Evans (eds) *Beyond educational reform*, Buckingham: Open University Press.

Marquardt, M. (1999) 'Action learning, info-line', *Organisational Development*, 97(4): 1–16.

Marquardt, M. (2004) 'Harnessing the power of action learning', *TD*, June: 26–32.

Marsick, V. (2002) 'Exploring the many meanings of action learning and action reflective learning; earning while learning in global leadership', *The Volvo MiL partnership*, Sweden: MiL Publishers.

Miller, P. (2003) 'Workplace learning by action learning: a practical example', *Journal of Workplace Learning*, 15(1): 14–24.

Mills, G. E. (2000) *Action research: a guide for the teacher researcher*, Columbus, OH: Merrill.

Mishler, E. (1990) 'Validation in inquiry-guided research: the role of exemplars in narrative studies', *Harvard Educational Review*, 90(4): 415–42.

New South Wales Department of Education and Training (NSW DET) (2003) 'Quality teaching in NSW public schools: a discussion paper', Sydney: Professional Support and Curriculum Directorate, NSW DET.

Newman, M. (2006) *Teaching defiance: stories and strategies for activist educators*, San Francisco, CA: Jossey-Bass.

Nias, J. (1995) 'Unpublished portrayal of Curl Curl North primary school', Sydney: Innovative Links Program, University of Technology.

Noddings, N. and Witherell, C. (1991) *Epilogue: themes remembered and foreseen*, New York: Teachers College Press.

Pedler, M. (2008) *Action learning for managers*, England: Gower Publishing.

Ponte, P. and Smit, B. (eds) (2008) *The quality of practitioner research: reflections on the position of the researcher and the researched*, Rotterdam: Sense Publishers.

Putnam, R. and Borko, H. (1997) 'Teacher learning: implications of new views of cognition', in B. J. Biddle (ed.) *International handbook of teachers and teaching*, Dordrecht, The Netherlands: Kluwer Academic Press.

Putnam, R. and Borko, H. (2000) 'What do new views of knowledge and thinking have to say about research on teacher learning?', *Educational Researcher*, 29(1): 4–15.

Ramsey, G. (2000) 'Quality matters', Review of teacher education in NSW, Sydney: NSW DET.

Reid, M. (1994) 'Action learning: a set within a set at MCB University Press', *Training and Development Methods*, 8(1): 101–10.

Retallick, J. A. (1997) 'Workplace learning and the school as a learning organisation', in R. J. King, D. M. Hill and J. A. Retallick (eds) *Exploring professional development in education*, Wentworth Falls, NSW: Social Science Press.

Revans, R. W. (1945) 'Plans for recruitment, education and training for the coalmining industry', Report commissioned by the Mining Association of Great Britain, London, October.

Revans, R. W. (1982a) *The origins and growth of action learning*, London: Chartwell-Bratt.

Revans, R. W. (1982b) 'What is action learning?', *Journal of Management Development*, 1(3): 64–75.

Revans, R. W. (1983a) 'Action learning: its terms and character', *Management Decision*, 21(1).

Revans, R. W. (1983b) *The ABC of action learning*, Bromley: Chartwell-Bratt.

Reynolds, R., McCormack, A. and Ferguson-Patrick, K. (2005) 'University/school partnerships: journeys of three academic partners', Paper presented at Australian Association for Research in Education Annual Conference, University of Western Sydney, Parramatta.

Richardson, V. (1994) 'Teacher inquiry as professional staff development', in S. Hollingsworth (ed.) *Teacher research and educational reform*, Chicago: University of Chicago Press, 186–203.

Robinson, M. (2001) 'It works, but is it action learning?', *Education and Training*, 43(2): 62–4.

Russell, T. and Bullock, S. (1999) 'Discovering our professional knowledge as teachers: critical dialogues about learning from experience', in J. Loughran (ed.) *Researching teaching: methodologies and practices for understanding pedagogy*, London/Philadelphia: Falmer Press.

Sachs, J. (2003) *The activist teaching profession*, Buckingham and Philadelphia: Open University Press.

Sachs, J. and Logan, L. (1990) 'Control or development? A study of inservice education', *Journal of Curriculum Studies*, 22(5): 473–81.

Sagor, R. (2000) *Guiding school improvement with action research*, Alexandria, VA: ASCD.

Sarason, S. (1990) *The predictable failure of educational reform: can we change course before it is too late?*, San Francisco, CA: Jossey-Bass.

Schlesinger, E. (1991) 'Quality service in New Zealand', in M. Pedler (ed.) *Action learning in practice*, Aldershot: Gower Publishing.

Schmoker, M. (2005) 'No turning back: the ironclad case for professional learning communities', in R. DuFour, R. Eaker and R. DuFour (eds) *On common ground: the power of professional learning communities*, Bloomington, IN: Solution Tree.

Schön, D. A. (1983) *The reflective practitioner: how professionals think in action*. New York: Basic Books.

Schön, D. A. (1987) *Educating the reflective practitioner: toward a new design for teaching and learning in the professions*, San Francisco, CA: Jossey-Bass.

Schön, D. A. (ed.) (1991) *The reflective turn,* New York: Teachers College Press.

Schuck, S., Aubusson, P. and Buchanan, J. (2008) 'Enhancing teacher education practice through professional learning conversations', *European Journal of Teacher Education*, 31(2): 215–27.

Senge, P. M. (1990) *The fifth discipline: the art and practice of the learning organization*, New York: Currency Doubleday.

Senge, P., Cambron-McCabe, N., Lucas, T., Smith, B., Dutton, J. and Kleiner, A. (2000) *Schools that learn: a fifth discipline fieldbook*, New York: Currency Doubleday.

Sergiovanni, T. J. (1999) 'Leadership and excellence in schooling: excellent schools need freedom within boundaries', in T. J. Sergiovanni (ed.) *Rethinking leadership*, Thousand Oaks, CA: Corwin Press.

Sheffield, R., Hackling, M. and Goodrum, D. (2004) 'Mapping changes in teachers' practice during a professional learning program: Collaborative Australian Secondary

Science Program (CASSP)', Paper presented at the Conference of the Australasian Science Education Research Association, Armidale, Australia, July.

Siskin, L. S. (1994) *Realms of knowledge: academic departments in high schools*, London: Falmer Press.

Smith, D. L. (1995) 'Fostering reflection in student teachers: on the efficacy of the strategy of critical friend peer interviews', Paper presented at the Second National Cross Faculty Practicum Conference, Gold Coast, Queensland, Australia, 3–6 February.

Smith, D. L. (1999) 'The what, why and how of reflective practice in teacher education', Keynote address presented to Education Faculty Staff, Auckland College of Education, New Zealand.

Smith, D. L. (2007) Unpublished materials for use as a critical friend in action learning projects.

Smith, D. L. (2008a) Unpublished reflective scaffolds used in action learning projects.

Smith, D. L. (2008b) 'Sydney Catholic education research report', Unpublished report to Sydney Diocese CEO, September.

Smith, D. L. and Lovat, T. (2003) *Curriculum: action on reflection*, 4th edn, Melbourne: Thomson.

Smith, S., Smith, P. and Cupitt, C. (2007) 'Sustainability in schools: a good place to start', *Independent Education*, 37(2): 16–17.

Spillane, J., Halverson, R. and Diamond, J. (2001) 'Investigating school leadership practice: a distributed perspective', *Educational Researcher*, 30(3): 23–8.

Stenhouse, L. (1979) *What is action-research?*, Norwich: University of East Anglia.

Turner, M. and Bash, L. (1999) *Sharing expertise in teacher education*, London: Cassell.

Valli, L. (1992) *Reflective teacher education: cases and critiques*, Albany: University of New York Press.

van Manen, M. (1992) *Researching lived experiences. Human science for an action sensitive pedagogy*, London and Ontario: The Althouse Press.

Wade, S. and Hammick, M. (1999) 'Action learning circles: action learning in theory and practice', *Teaching in Higher Education*, 4(2): 163–78.

Walford, G. (2005) 'Research ethical guidelines and anonymity', *International Journal of Research and Method in Education*, 28(1): 83–93.

Weinstein, K. (1998) 'Action learning in the UK', *Performance Improvement Quarterly*, 11(1): 149–67.

Wenger, E. C. (1998) *Communities of practice: learning meaning and identity*, Cambridge: Cambridge University Press.

Wenger, E. C. and Snyder, W. M. (2000) 'Communities of practice: the organisational frontier', *Harvard Business Review*, 78(1): 139–45.

Wenger, E., McDermott, R. and Snyder, W. M. (2002) *Cultivating communities of practice*, Boston, MA: Harvard Business School Press.

Wertsch, J. V. and Rupert, L. J. (1993) 'The authority of cultural tools in a sociocultural approach to mediated agency', *Cognition and Instruction*, 11: 227–40.

Winkless, T. (1991) 'Doctors as managers', in M. Pedler (ed.) *Action learning in practice*, Aldershot: Gower Publishing (available online).

Wise, A. E., Darling-Hammond, L., McLaughlin, M. W. and Bernstein, H. T. (1984) *Teacher evaluation: a study of effective practice*, Santa Monica, CA: Rand Corporation.

Yeatman, A. and Sachs, J. (1995) *Making the links: a formative evaluation of the first year of the innovative links between universities and schools for teacher professional development*, Perth, WA: Murdoch University.

York-Barr, J. and Duke, K. (2004) 'What do we know about teacher leadership? Findings from two decades of scholarship', *Review of Educational Research*, 74(3): 255–316.

Zeichner, K. (2003) 'Teacher research as professional development for P-12 educators in the USA', *Educational Action Research*, 11(2): 301–25.

Zuber-Skerritt, O. (1993) 'Improving learning and teaching through action learning and action research', *Higher Education Research and Development*, 12(1): 45–58.

Zuber-Skerritt, O. (2002) 'A model for designing action learning and action research programs', *The Learning Organisation*, 9(4): 143–9.

Index